"In post-industrial Pittsburgh, smoke did not get in our eyes, but an abundance of stunning architecture did. The density of fine buildings—many by celebrated designers, many not—could be tops in the nation. (H. H. Richardson's Allegheny County Courthouse and Jail struck me as the most sublime of the lot.) Plus, the city's hills let one view them from all sorts of angles and distances. To gaze at downtown's skyline from atop the Duquesne Incline … was to feel very lucky indeed."

—Arnold Berke, Executive Editor,
Preservation (January/February 2007)

Look up when you walk Downtown. You'll be surprised by what you see.

"[This guidebook] provides sightseers with everything they need—color photos of the buildings and structural adornments ... addresses, architects, construction dates, walking directions, and contextual information ... . But perhaps the best bit of sightseer information is the mantra [stated in the caption above]."

—STEPHEN KNEZOVICH, CONTRIBUTING EDITOR,
PITTSBURGH MAGAZINE (FEBRUARY 2009)

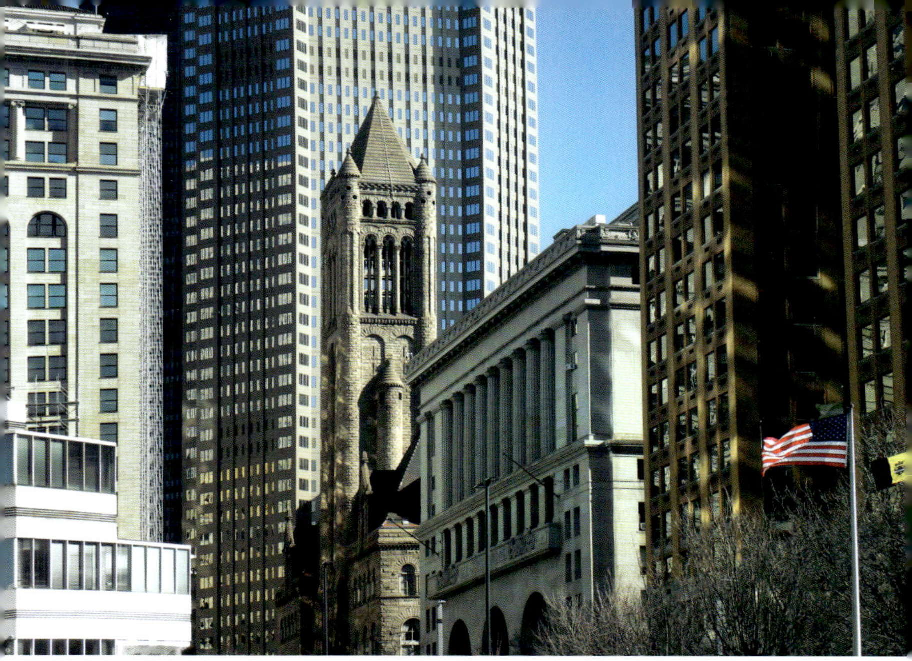

The quality of H. H. Richardson's Allegheny County Courthouse tower is apparent and undiminished among the ever-taller skyscrapers on Grant Street. "It is one of the world's great towers," wrote architectural historian Walter C. Kidney.

EXPLORING PITTSBURGH
A DOWNTOWN WALKING TOUR

Pittsburgh History & Landmarks Foundation
100 West Station Square Drive, Suite 450
Pittsburgh, PA 15219-1134
412-471-5808
www.phlf.org

© 2018 by Pittsburgh History & Landmarks Foundation
All rights reserved.

Printed in the United States of America

Editor: Louise King Sturgess

Editorial assistance: Maria Brown, Christine McClure, Amanda Seim, Frank Stroker, Albert M. Tannler, and David J. Vater, RA

Design: Greg Pytlik

ISBN-978-0-9969372-2-1

Library of Congress Control Number: 2018940566

Exploring Pittsburgh is typeset in Minion with Formata subheads. It was printed on 80# McCoy Silk Text by Migliozzi Printing Services and J.B. Kreider Printing, Pittsburgh, PA.

Acknowledgements

The text in this guidebook is drawn primarily from major books published by the Pittsburgh History & Landmarks Foundation *(see Bibliography, page 95)*. Laurie Cohen assisted in editing the first and second editions of this guidebook, previously titled *Whirlwind Walk: Architecture and Urban Spaces in Downtown Pittsburgh* (PHLF, 2008 and 2011).

We thank Todd Wilson, PE, PHLF trustee and co-author of *Pittsburgh's Bridges* (Arcadia Publishing, 2015), for providing information for the Portal Bridge caption on page 77.

We thank the Green Building Alliance for providing the information for "What's 'Green' Downtown?" *(see pages 85–88)*.

Exploring Pittsburgh:
A Downtown Walking Tour
is supported by generous contributions from
the Carl Wood Brown Named Fund
at the Pittsburgh History & Landmarks Foundation
and from Bernard J. McCrory, Jr.,
in memory of Beth Buckholtz (1960–2017),
who helped design many of
PHLF's publications.

PHLF thanks Downtown Pittsburgh
building owners
for welcoming our tour groups
throughout the year.

Contents

Introduction ix
   Excerpts from "The Overlooked City" 1
   Architectural History: In Brief 3

Downtown Walking Tour 7
   Tour Sites and Map 8
   Buildings and Places 11
   A Final Note 79

Appendix 81
   Downtown Museums and More 83
   What's "Green" Downtown? 85
   Publications and Tours 91
   Illustration Sources 93
   Bibliography 95
   Index 97

Opposite: Look up to see the domed vaults of Guastavino tile over the Grant Street entrance portico of the City-County Building.

Introduction

City-County Building (1915–17): allegorical frieze by New York sculptor Charles Keck, with the crest of the City of Pittsburgh (above). The City crest is based on the family coat of arms of Sir William Pitt the Elder, the British statesman for whom Pittsburgh was named in 1758.

Three rivers frame "a narrow triangular spit of land onto which the skyscraper core of the city is crammed like a fairy tale of vertical steel, aluminum, and glass," writes urban designer David Lewis. The Monongahela River (right), flowing *north*, and the Allegheny River (left), flowing south, meet at Pittsburgh's Point to form the Ohio River that flows west to the Mississippi.

Excerpts from
"The Overlooked City"

Pittsburgh is a city waiting to be discovered and explored. Is it a "great" city? No, not yet. I would say it has the makings of a great city. But whether it is a great city in the making depends, not on the past, but on the future, on us, and on Pittsburgh's future citizens.

Great cities are accretions, added to and modified over centuries, worked and reworked by generation after generation of citizens, until they become a precise and intricate physical and cultural language, as capable of profundity, beauty, and sensitivity of utterance as any music or poetry. A great city is, in fact, the artwork of its people. …

Demolitions still go on today, of course, but we are all much more sensitive to the issues now. We are beginning to understand what European and Asian cities have known for centuries—that old buildings are much more than just obsolete structures in the physical sense. They are the custodians of our cultural continuity as a city and as a community. …

We are beginning to see that cities are, in an important sense, living and evolving organisms. Their past is the foundation of their future. There is no starting all over again from scratch. …

Pittsburgh truly is a city composed of villages. The Golden Triangle, in spite of the size of its new buildings, is the scale of a village. Every part of it is within walking distance. And it has churches, a park, squares, and riverbanks. …

—David Lewis, urban designer
"The Overlooked City," from
the Carnegie Magazine Map of Pittsburgh, 1975

Historic buildings on Fort Pitt Boulevard constructed between 1850 and 1890—after Pittsburgh's Great Fire of 1845—give a human scale to the city.

Architectural History: In Brief

Strategically located at the forks of the Ohio River, Pittsburgh was founded by the British on November 25, 1758. The wilderness outpost became the "Gateway to the West," then the "Workshop of the World," and now the city we know today of 55 square miles, populated by 305,704 people (2010 census). About 2.3 million people live in the Greater Pittsburgh region, an area including Allegheny, Armstrong, Beaver, Butler, Fayette, Washington, and Westmoreland counties.

Throughout its history, Pittsburgh has been known for its great natural beauty, resources, and industry. The hills—rich in coal, shale, sandstone, and limestone—were formed over 300 million years ago. Some 12,000 years ago glacial action shoved the Allegheny, Monongahela, and Ohio rivers into their present courses. People have inhabited this region for thousands of years, but it is only in the last two centuries that the face of the landscape has changed significantly. Now bridges span the rivers and valleys, tunnels pierce the hills, and the towers of Downtown dominate the urban landscape. With changes in elevation of 400 feet and more, Pittsburgh is a city in three dimensions.

Although Pittsburgh was founded in the 18th century, very little from that time remains, aside from the Fort Pitt Block House of 1764 in Point State Park and the street plan of 1784, laid out by George Woods and Thomas Vickroy for the heirs of William Penn.

Many significant 19th- and 20th-century buildings have survived. Of the 19th century prior to the Great Fire of 1845, there is only one building left for certain: the Greek Revival Burke's Building of 1836, on Fourth Avenue. A few simple buildings erected after the Fire remain in the 100 block of Market Street and in other places. Three tiny old houses of c. 1850 still cluster at Strawberry and Montour Ways. On Fort Pitt Boulevard, a handsome block of Victorian buildings from

Introduction

1850 and after survives; these give a human scale to the city as newer buildings rise beyond. Liberty Avenue has a large concentration of Victorian commercial architecture, too, and Penn Avenue is distinguished by a fine collection of early 20th-century commercial buildings. Among the close-built streets are special open spaces such as Market Square (originally laid out in 1784), Gateway Center, Mellon Square, PPG Plaza, Katz Plaza, BNY Mellon Green, PNC Firstside Park, and PNC Triangle Park.

The Golden Triangle—a term frequently used in the early 20th century referencing "the wealth of downtown banks and corporations and the thriving commercial climate," according to author Martin Aurand—once had a boat yard, foundries, and an assortment of rail lines and train stations. But zoning in 1923, the urban renewal that began around 1950, and more than two centuries of continuous growth and change have transformed the Downtown area into a compact neighborhood of businesses, government agencies, cultural and academic institutions, shops, restaurants, public spaces, and residences once again.

Beyond the Golden Triangle, the region's spectacular landscape contains many architectural treasures. General John Neville's "Woodville" in Collier Township is our principal link with 18th-century American life and architecture. The Croghan-Schenley ballroom and anteroom, said to be the finest surviving Northern Greek Revival interior in the country, and elements from A. W. N. Pugin's House of Commons preserved in the English Nationality Room, are both located within the University of Pittsburgh's Cathedral of Learning. Evergreen Hamlet's Gothic Revival "cottages" comprise one of the first American suburbs, while Craftsman homes in Thornburg were adapted from early 20th-century California houses. H. H. Richardson's Emmanuel Episcopal Church and Modern American Gothic churches by Ralph Adams Cram and Bertram Goodhue are located in various city

Introduction

neighborhoods. Charles J. Connick, America's leading stained-glass artist of the 20th century who was educated and trained in Pittsburgh, designed windows for ten historic landmarks in and near Pittsburgh. Walter Gropius and Marcel Breuer designed the Frank House, a masterpiece of modernism, and there are buildings by Ludwig Mies van der Rohe, Richard Meier, Robert Venturi, Philip Johnson, and Michael Graves. In addition, the work of important architects who designed extensively in the Pittsburgh area—Longfellow, Alden & Harlow; Henry Hornbostel; Frederick G. Scheibler, Jr.; Benno Janssen; and Taliesin Fellows Cornelia Brierly and Peter Berndtson—have now been explored in major books.

"Pittsburgh grew with a rapidity and a grandeur unmatched by any city in the old world," writes urban designer David Lewis—and the work of building and rebuilding goes on.

October 2017: Point Park University's Pittsburgh Playhouse on Forbes Avenue in Downtown Pittsburgh is shown under construction, about one year before its opening in August 2018.

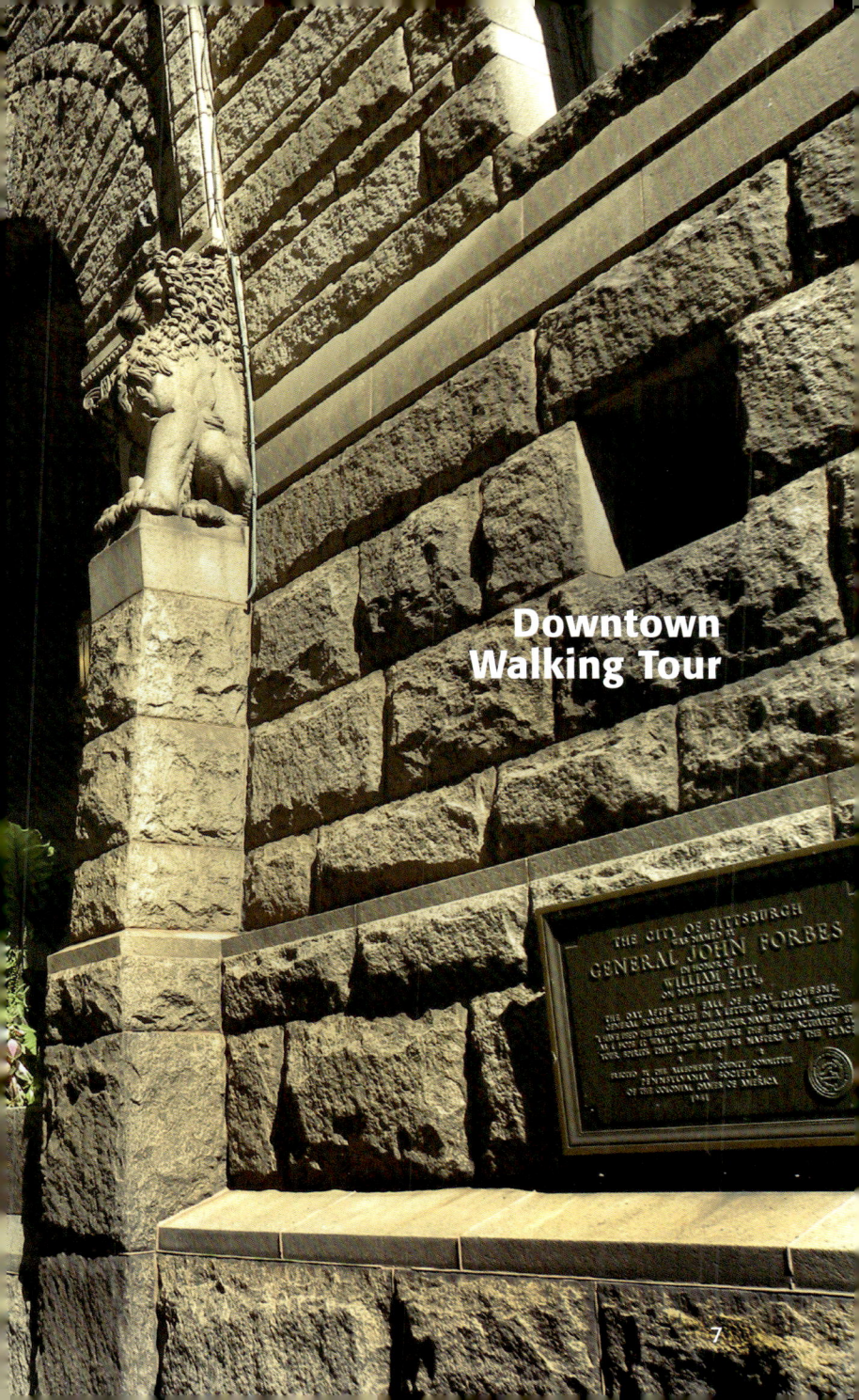
Downtown Walking Tour

OUR SITES AND MAP

1. Allegheny County Courthouse and Jail
2. City-County Building
3. Grant Building
4. PNC Firstside Center and Park
5. One Oxford Centre
6. Frick Building
7. Union Trust Building
8. Omni William Penn Hotel
9. BNY Mellon Center
10. U.S. Steel Tower
11. First Lutheran Church
12. Joseph F. Weis Jr. United States Courthouse
13. The Pennsylvanian
14. Drury Plaza Hotel Pittsburgh Downtown
15. Gulf Tower
16. Koppers Building
17. Verizon Building
18. Smithfield United Church
19. Allegheny HYP Club
20. The Residences at the Historic Alcoa Building
21. Mellon Square
22. Trinity Cathedral
23. First Presbyterian Church
24. Duquesne Club
25. Granite Building
26. Wood Street Station and Wood Street Galleries
27. Midtown Towers
28. Cultural District
29. 300 Sixth Avenue Building
30. Two PNC Plaza
31. One PNC Plaza
32. The Tower at PNC Plaza
33. 400 Block, Wood Street
34. Point Park University Center
35. CVS/pharmacy
36. Market Square Place
37. Market Square
38. Market at Fifth
39. Buhl Building
40. Three PNC Plaza and PNC Triangle Park
41. Burke's Building
42. Fourth Avenue Historic District
43. PPG Place
44. St. Mary of Mercy Church
45. Four Gateway Center
46. Gateway Center One, Two, and Three
47. Wyndham Grand Pittsburgh Downtown
48. Point State Park

Exploring Pittsburgh

D. H. Burnham & Company's Frick Building (1901–02)—gray and Neo-Classical—confronts H. H. Richardson's Romanesque masterpiece, the Allegheny County Courthouse and Jail (1884–88).

Buildings and Places

General Notes:

1. The walking tour route is highlighted on the map on pages 8–9.
2. If a city is not given with the architect's name, then the architect's office was, or is, located in Pittsburgh.
3. Some artists and their artwork are mentioned in the text; a comprehensive descriptive inventory can be found in Pittsburgh Art in Public Places: Downtown Walking Tour *(Office of Public Art, 2016).*
4. Sites designated with asterisks* have lobbies or other interior spaces that are open to the public and are worth seeing. Most of the sites so designated are open during the business week and some are also open on the weekends.

Begin at 436 Grant Street, Pittsburgh, PA 15219, and walk south. The Allegheny County Courthouse and former Jail are open each business day, from 9:00 a.m. to 4:00 p.m. Visitors must go through security to enter the Allegheny County Courthouse, the former Jail (entrances on Ross Street and Fifth Avenue), and the City-County Building (site 2). Sites 1 through 12, and 14 through 16, face Grant Street.

1. Allegheny County Courthouse and Jail*

436 Grant Street
Henry Hobson Richardson (Brookline, MA), architect,
1884–88; later alterations by others

H. H. Richardson's Allegheny County Courthouse and former Jail are the most important of Pittsburgh's great buildings. They introduced Pittsburgh to a more lucid, compositionally unified architecture than it had known for decades. At a time when American architects usually looked to Classical precedents, Richardson adapted 11th-century Romanesque forms to create a powerful new style for America. "The Court-house is the most magnificent and imposing of his works," wrote Richardson biographer Mariana G. S. Van Rensselaer, "yet it is the most logical and quiet. It is the most somber and severe, yet it is the most original … ."

Richardson was the first American architect of international significance. When he died on April 27, 1886 at the age of 47, many of his finest buildings were nearing completion in the East and Midwest: in the Boston area, Buffalo, Chicago, Cincinnati, Detroit, St. Louis, Washington, D.C., and Pittsburgh. On his deathbed, Richardson is reported to have said of the Allegheny County Courthouse and Jail: "If they honor me for the pigmy things I have already done, what will they say when they see Pittsburgh finished." Architectural historian James F. O'Gorman calls the Allegheny County Courthouse and Jail "without doubt his most impressive surviving monument."

Although it is hard to imagine today, the western end of Grant's Hill, "the Hump," penetrated the Golden Triangle between Forbes and Sixth avenues and was about 60 feet high. In 1836 and again in 1844 and 1847, efforts were made to cut down the Hump. Between 1911 and 1913, Grant, Ross, and nearby streets were lowered for the last time to improve access for public safety and transit vehicles. After the final lowering of Grant Street, an exterior staircase set over three new ground-floor entrances to the Courthouse was erected. In 1926, however, Grant Street was widened and the exterior staircase was removed. Richardson's original Courthouse entrances then became arched windows above new doorways created by Allegheny County Architect Stanley L. Roush, leading to a basement vestibule-and-stair system covered by Guastavino-tile vaulting. (The lightweight structural-tile system was introduced to the United States in 1888 by Barcelona engineer Rafael Guastavino.) The Courthouse lions, on level with the original entrances, are now about 15 feet above street level *(see photo on pages 6–7)*.

Courthouse, Grant Street: March 28, 1913

Enter the Courthouse and go through security. Walk up the basement stair to the first floor to see Richardson's grand staircase and the murals from the 1930s by Vincent Nesbert.

Exit into the courtyard to see the fountain (constructed when the courtyard was redesigned in 1976–77); two plaques; and a magnificent view of the building façade and Courthouse tower, the tallest in Pittsburgh when completed in 1888.

The Courthouse is connected to the former Jail by the "Bridge of Sighs" over Ross Street. When the Jail was closed in 1995 due to overcrowding, IKM Incorporated sensitively converted the building into the Family Division of the Allegheny County Court of Common Pleas. The building reopened in 2000 and includes a Jail Museum.

H. H. Richardson's Allegheny County Courthouse and Jail were designated a National Historic Landmark in 1976. Restoration continues at the Courthouse through the leadership of the County Executive, in consultation with the Pittsburgh History & Landmarks Foundation.

2. City-County Building*

*414 Grant Street
Edward B. Lee, and Palmer, Hornbostel & Jones, associated architects, 1915–17*

Henry Hornbostel (1867–1961), who had come from New York City to Pittsburgh in 1904 to design the Carnegie Technical Schools (now

Carnegie Mellon University), was the master behind this visionary design. The style feels Classical—vaulted, columned, measured—though the detailing is very largely original. The Grant Street entrance portico has Guastavino-tile vaulting in a fish-scale pattern.

The ground-floor corridor is one of Pittsburgh's great interior spaces. The 43-foot-tall by 150-foot-long passage is lined with bronze-encased columns. A life-size portrait bust of Sir William Pitt the Elder (1708–1778), the British statesman for whom Pittsburgh was named, is from 1922. The sculptor was Glasgow-born Sir William Reid Dick, Sculptor Ordinaire to King George VI and later Elizabeth II. Elevator doors show figures holding the three Allegheny County Courthouses and the three Pittsburgh City Halls, past and present. The windows at the corridor ends have double thicknesses of glass, with the floor plates between them, so that people passing from side to side seem to be striding on air.

3. Grant Building

310–330 Grant Street
Henry Hornbostel, architect; Eric Fisher Wood, associated architect, 1927–30

At 460 feet and 40 floors, the Grant Building was briefly the tallest in Pittsburgh and was state-of-the-art for its time. An inept renovation beginning in the 1960s resulted in the removal of the original entrance lamps, window sash, and pinnacles. But the 23-foot beacon,

Downtown Walking Tour

the largest in the world when installed, continues to flash "Pittsburgh" in Morse code. All the original components were made in Pittsburgh, including 32 pyrex tubes and 416 lineal feet of neon. Huntington National Bank opened a regional office in the Grant Building in 2011 and changed the red-orange neon beacon to green.

Continue south on Grant Street to First Avenue.

4. PNC Firstside Center and Park

500 First Avenue
Astorino, architect, 2000;
landscape architect, 2007

Located near the First Avenue "T" (transit) station and a riverfront biking and hiking trail, PNC Firstside Center was the nation's first financial institution to be certified under the LEED (Leadership in Energy and Environmental Design) building rating system *(see page 85)*. Light wells in the elegant, five-story building bring natural light into the interior, exposing 90 percent of floor areas to natural light and outside

views. A hybrid air-distribution system provides improved control, employee comfort, and energy savings.

Across First Avenue is **PNC Firstside Park**, bordered by Grant Street, Second Avenue, and Ross Street. It is privately owned by PNC but is open to the public. Astorino's landscape architects, led by Christine Astorino, designed the park using

native and adapted plant species, drip-irrigation for high-water efficiency, and materials from local suppliers. The park includes more than 100 trees (red maples, white birches, sweet bay magnolias, and flowering crabapple, among many others), perennials, and ornamental grasses. Follow the spiral paths to find notable sculptures of monkeys, rabbits, and frogs by Albert Guibara, and inspirational quotes from Confucius, Helen Keller, Mister Rogers, and Martin Luther King, Jr. In 2009, Clement Meadmore's spiral steel sculpture of 1977, "Up and Away," was relocated from One PNC Plaza to PNC Firstside Park.

Cross to the west side of Grant Street and walk north.

PNC Firstside Park, in November 2009, with a view toward the former red-brick Salvation Army building of 1924 and 1930 (Thomas Pringle, architect) that was transformed into the Distrikt Hotel Pittsburgh in 2017.

Downtown Walking Tour

5. One Oxford Centre*

*301 Grant Street
Hellmuth, Obata & Kassabaum
(New York), architects, 1983*

This 45-story skyscraper was built as a cluster of octagons to maximize the number of corner offices. An elegant entrance atrium leads to a food hall, collaborative work spaces, and the Rivers Club.

6. Frick Building*

*437 Grant Street
D. H. Burnham & Company
(Chicago), architects, 1901–02*

Henry Clay Frick (1849–1919) —Pittsburgh's "Coke King," Chairman of Carnegie Steel, and philanthropist—made a number of major real-estate investments that resulted in construction of a close-set group of buildings in the Grant Street area: the Frick Building, Frick Annex (now the Allegheny Building), Union Arcade (now Union Trust Building), and the William Penn Hotel.

Frick Annex (left) and Frick Building (center)

In the Frick Building, the earliest of these, he created a personal monument and the location of his own office. "With its steel frame enclosed in a severe Neo-Classical masonry envelop," wrote architectural historian James D. Van Trump, the Frick Building "marks the emergence of the great slab skyscraper in Pittsburgh. Massive and powerful in both form

Continued on page 20

17

"Pittsburgh especially is a city of monuments to its great industrialists who left behind them not only steel mills, factories, and banks, but also a number of huge buildings which perpetuate their names. [Mellon], Frick, Carnegie, Oliver, and Phipps resound in the city's architectural as well as its financial annals. Like the princes of the Renaissance, the masters of these great fortunes loved to build. In steel, marble, and granite is memorialized much of the history of Pittsburgh's Age of Moguls.

"In their way, these men were as colorful and forceful as the conquerors of the past, and their achievements

Grand interiors: the Frick Building (opposite), the Henry W. Oliver Building (top left), and the impressive marble lobby and grand staircase of the Renaissance Pittsburgh Hotel (top right, shown before an interior remodeling of 2009).

were vital to the commercial development not only of Pittsburgh, but the nation as well. They had consolidated their triumphs in the business world and building was the best way of memorializing their conquests. …

"Within the Triangle, these structures tended to develop in colonies. Each industrialist carved out a tract of his own—H. C. Frick in the area near Richardson's Courthouse, Henry W. Oliver along Oliver Avenue, and Henry Phipps beside the Allegheny River."

—James D. Van Trump
"The Skyscraper as Monument,"
The Charette (43:4), April 1963

Continued from page 17

and detail, eminently suited to the spirit of the city and the time, there seems to be little doubt that H. C. Frick … intended it as a monument to his financial might." The 21-story building put an end to the 14-year dominance of the Pittsburgh skyline by the Courthouse directly across the street.

The Frick Building was designed by D. H. Burnham & Company. Daniel Burnham (1846–1912) planned the 1893 World's Columbian Exposition in Chicago and was an advocate of the City Beautiful movement. Of the 11 executed (and documented) designs for Pittsburgh by D. H. Burnham & Company, the Frick Building is one of only seven survivors.

Inside the Frick Building lobby are bronze lions (1902) by Alexander Phimister Proctor; an opalescent glass window, *Fortune* (1902), by John La Farge (who invented the process); and a marble bust of Frick (1923) by Malvina Hoffman.

Once outside, look up at the Fifth Avenue corner of the Frick Building to see a thin bronze marker that reads:

"Street grade prior to 1912." Between 1911 and 1913, the final cut was made in Grant's Hill and about 15 feet of earth was scraped away to create a more level street plan. As a result, facings of both the Courthouse and the Frick Building had to be extended downward, and their interior plans adjusted.

7. Union Trust Building*

501 Grant Street
Frederick J. Osterling, architect, 1915–17

Commissioned by Henry Clay Frick, this is one of Pittsburgh's most admired buildings. Designed by Frederick J. Osterling (1865–1934), who enlarged Richardson's Jail in 1904–08, the Flemish Gothic Revival building draws inspiration from the Municipal Hall at Leuven, Belgium, dating to the 15th century. The twin rooftop structures now house heating, ventilating and cooling systems, although local legend suggested that one was a chapel since the second St. Paul Cathedral had been located on this site until the early 1900s.

Originally called the Union Arcade and described as the world's largest shopping mall, the massive building was filled with 240 shops, facing two four-story open arcade spaces, and more than 700 offices. In 1923, it became the Union Trust Building, and the upper three floors of the shops running parallel to Grant Street were enclosed, reducing the openness of the interior.

In 2014, The Davis Companies (whose CEO and founder, Jonathan G. Davis, is a Pittsburgh native) purchased the Union Trust Building and initiated a $100 million restoration. Improvements included cleaning the exterior stone and lighting the façade at night; extensively repairing and restoring the mansard roof using the original terra-cotta molds; restoring the bronze storefronts; and re-lighting the extraordinary stained-glass dome atop the 150½-foot-high rotunda. Go inside, walk to the center, and look up!

Exploring Pittsburgh

8. Omni William Penn Hotel*

*555 Grant Street; main entrance: 530 William Penn Place
Janssen & Abbott, architects, 1914–16; Janssen & Cocken, architects,
1926–29; Urban Room, Joseph Urban (New York), 1929*

View from Mellon Square

Deep light courts in this classic big-city hotel allow the maximum number of guest rooms to have natural light and outdoor views. Inside, the hotel is distinguished by a gracious first-floor lobby and, on the 17th floor, by an impressive ballroom and the Urban Room, one of the last Art Deco interiors designed and decorated by Joseph Urban (1872–1933). The exuberant room of gold-trimmed black marble and Carrara glass, decorated with exotic murals (in need of some restoration), is the sole survivor of the hotel reception rooms and supper clubs designed by Urban between 1927 and 1933.

During a $22 million renovation in 2004, many of the building's original elements were restored and the main lobby was redecorated. A Prohibition-era bar, The Speakeasy, is tucked beneath the hotel lobby.

9. BNY Mellon Center

*500 Grant Street
Welton Becket & Associates (Los Angeles), architects,
with Celli-Flynn Associates, 1983*

This 54-story skyscraper, the second tallest in Pittsburgh at 725 feet, was the only element built in a project conceived to include a health club, parking garage, hotel, and apartment

tower. The architects sited BNY Mellon Center (originally built for the Dravo Corporation) to allow a broadside view of H. H.

Above: the Palm Court and main lobby of the Omni William Penn Hotel.
Below: A mural in the hotel's Terrace Room, painted in 1950 by Andrew Karoly and Louis Szanto, commemorates the founding of Pittsburgh by British General John Forbes on November 25, 1758. George Washington, age 26, was there.

Richardson's Allegheny County Courthouse. The mansard roof of BNY Mellon Center pays homage to the Union Trust Building. The plaza sculpture is *Chairs for Six*, by Scott Burton (1986).

BNY Mellon Green, designed in 2002 by Burt Hill Kosar Rittelmann and MTR Landscape Architects, gives a campus feel to the BNY Mellon financial center complex and provides an amenity for Pittsburgh's central business district. A tree-lined promenade of rustic terrazzo and granite paving leads to a fountain designed by Cindy Tyler of MTR. BNY Mellon Green is adjacent to the Steel Plaza Station, one of four light rail "T" (transit) stations in Downtown Pittsburgh.

10. U.S. Steel Tower

600 Grant Street
Max Abramovitz, Charles H. Abbe, Harrison & Abramovitz (New York), architects, and United States Steel Innovations Committee, 1965–71

The collaborative design process between a prestigious New York firm and experts from within various United States Steel divisions, as well as outside consultants, led to an innovative building design, new construction techniques, and advances in various building systems such as air conditioning and fire proofing. When completed in 1971, the U.S. Steel Tower was the largest commercial high-rise office building in the world, with an acre of space on each of its 64 stories.

At 841 feet, U.S. Steel Tower was the tallest building between New York and Chicago until 1987, when One Liberty Place was completed in Philadelphia (945 feet). The skyscraper, seen from a distance overtopping Pittsburgh's hills, now bears the letters UPMC, since the nonprofit "University of Pittsburgh Medical Center" also is headquartered there. UPMC is the region's largest employer.

The U.S. Steel Tower has an exposed frame of USS Cor-Ten plate steel (a U.S. Steel patent). Originally developed for steel surfaces that could not be painted (such as rail cars or bridges), Cor-Ten is intrinsically resistant to atmospheric corrosion. The 18 supporting columns, rising the full 841 feet, are filled with a mixture of water, anti-freeze, and an anti-corrosive. The purpose of the fluid is to maintain a column temperature below a dangerous level during a fire. The triangular shape of the skyscraper was structurally innovative and echoes the shape of the Golden Triangle. Approximately 9,000 people work in the tower, and there are 54 elevator cars and 11,000 windows.

11. First Lutheran Church*

615 Grant Street
Andrew W. Peebles, architect, 1887–88

Born in Scotland, Andrew W. Peebles (c. 1835–1919) was active in Pittsburgh between 1871 and 1896. He was the only Pittsburgh architect invited to participate in the competition for the Allegheny County Courthouse and Jail, announced by the Commissioners in 1883, but he missed the deadline.

His First Lutheran Church was completed two months after H. H. Richardson's Courthouse. The Courthouse tower and the 170-foot spire of Peebles' picturesque sandstone Gothic Revival church dominated the area. Grant Street still had the air of a small-town Main Street, but taller, steel-framed buildings were soon to rise. Now overshadowed on all sides, the church maintains its dignity and purpose.

Inside are several notable objects: an altarpiece in the 15th-century Italian Renaissance style with mosaics; windows by S. S. Marshall & Company, one of the earliest of Pittsburgh's stained glass studios; a *Good Shepherd* window with over 500 square feet of opalescent glass, designed in 1898 by Frederick

Wilson of Tiffany Glass & Decorating Company; and a font in the form of a kneeling angel with a basin, a copy of one in Copenhagen by Bertel Thorvaldsen.

12. Joseph F. Weis Jr. United States Courthouse

700 Grant Street
Trowbridge & Livingston (New York), architects,
with James A. Wetmore (Washington, D.C.), 1932–34

Originally the Federal Courthouse and Post Office, this massive building with its 14 acres of floor space exhibits the restrained Neo-Classicism favored by the Federal Government in the 1930s. Its progenitor was Andrew W. Mellon (whose family sponsored the former Mellon Bank, the Gulf Building, and Mellon Square). The Federal courtrooms are decorated with murals by Howard Cook (1901–1980), Stuveysant Van Veen (1910–1977), and others.

Samuel Trowbridge (1862–1925) graduated from Columbia University's School of Architecture in 1886, attended the École des Beaux-Arts in Paris, and later apprenticed in the firm of George B. Post in New York. He established his partnership c. 1901 with Goodhue Livingston (1865–1931), who also attended Columbia and worked for Post.

During a $68 million renovation in 2004–05, the exterior stonework was cleaned, six new courtrooms were added in the original building light wells, and an atrium was constructed to allow natural light to illuminate the new third-floor lobby space and historic fourth-floor courtroom.

The Post Office closed in 2014. The next year, the building was renamed to honor Joseph F. Weis, Jr. (1923–2014), a decorated World War II combat veteran and one of the nation's most respected Federal appellate judges.

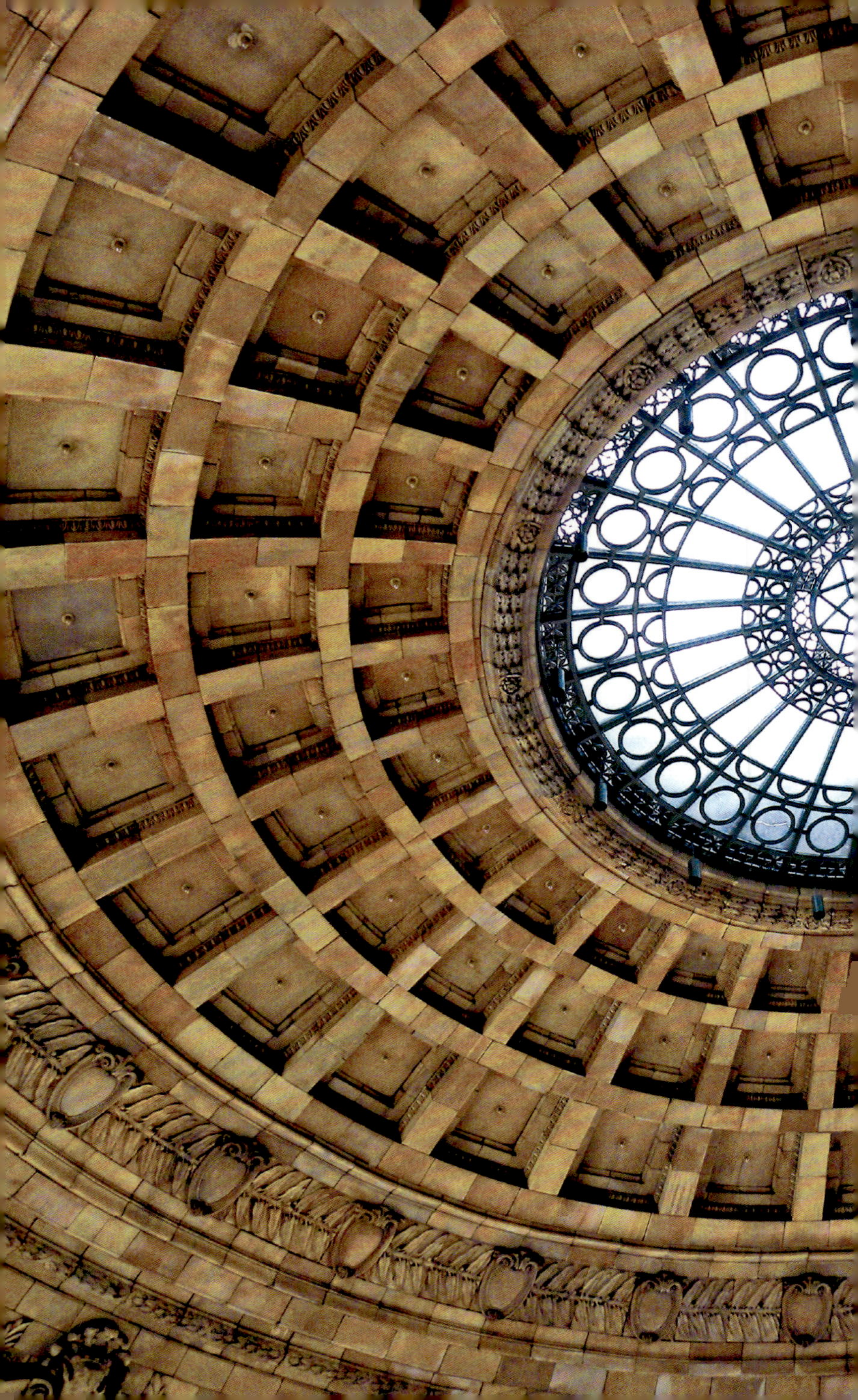

Continue along Grant Street until you can see site 13 in the distance.

13. The Pennsylvanian

*1100 Liberty Avenue
D. H. Burnham & Company (Chicago), architects, 1898–1903;
Bower Lewis Thrower (Philadelphia), architects for remodeling, 1988*

D. H. Burnham's second Pittsburgh commission was the grandest—the 12-story Union Station of the Pennsylvania Railroad. Faced in buff brick and elaborate terra-cotta ornamentation, the passenger train station evoked the Classicism of late-19th-century Paris. James D. Van Trump called the entrance shelter, known as the rotunda, "a pavilion of enchantment and light and a grotto of contrived, curvilinear shadows, endlessly fascinating."

In 1988, Union Station was remodeled as The Pennsylvanian, with offices on the lower floors and apartments above. The brick and the terra cotta were cleaned and repaired, and the rotunda skylight was restored and opened again. The rotunda arches are outlined in softly glowing carbon-filament bulbs, like those used in 1902. Amtrak maintains a station within the complex.

Return to Grant Street and Seventh Avenue to see sites 14, 15, and 16.

In the rotunda, Pittsburgh is spelled without the "h". In 1891, in order to standardize spellings nationwide, the U.S. Board on Geographic Names announced that Pittsburgh must drop its "h". After much public protest, Pittsburgh's "h" was restored in 1911.

Exploring Pittsburgh

14. Drury Plaza Hotel Pittsburgh Downtown*
745 Grant Street
Walker & Weeks (Cleveland), architects; Henry Hornbostel and Eric Fisher Wood, consulting architects, 1930–31; additions. Strada, architect for renovation and restoration, 2014–17

Originally designed for the Federal Reserve Bank of Cleveland, Pittsburgh Branch, this Art Deco building with white Georgia marble and decorative aluminum has been beautifully restored and renovated for the Drury Plaza Hotel. Inside, original Art Deco details and a painting of Downtown Pittsburgh in the late 1950s have been preserved in the lobby and bar area. The vaults in the basement have been transformed into meeting rooms; the former firing range is now an indoor pool and whirlpool; and a rooftop deck provides a welcome spot to enjoy city views.

Sculptor Henry Hering designed the decorative aluminum detailing on the exterior of the building. The three figures represent mining, agriculture, and commerce. The "4D" symbol in the grillwork refers to the Fourth District Federal Reserve Bank.

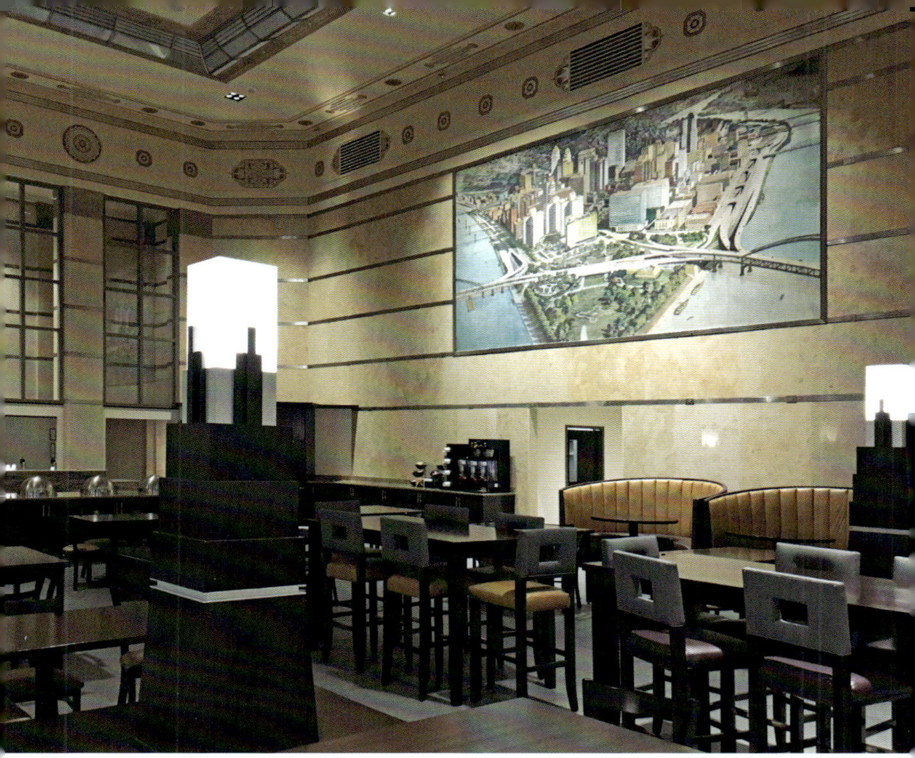

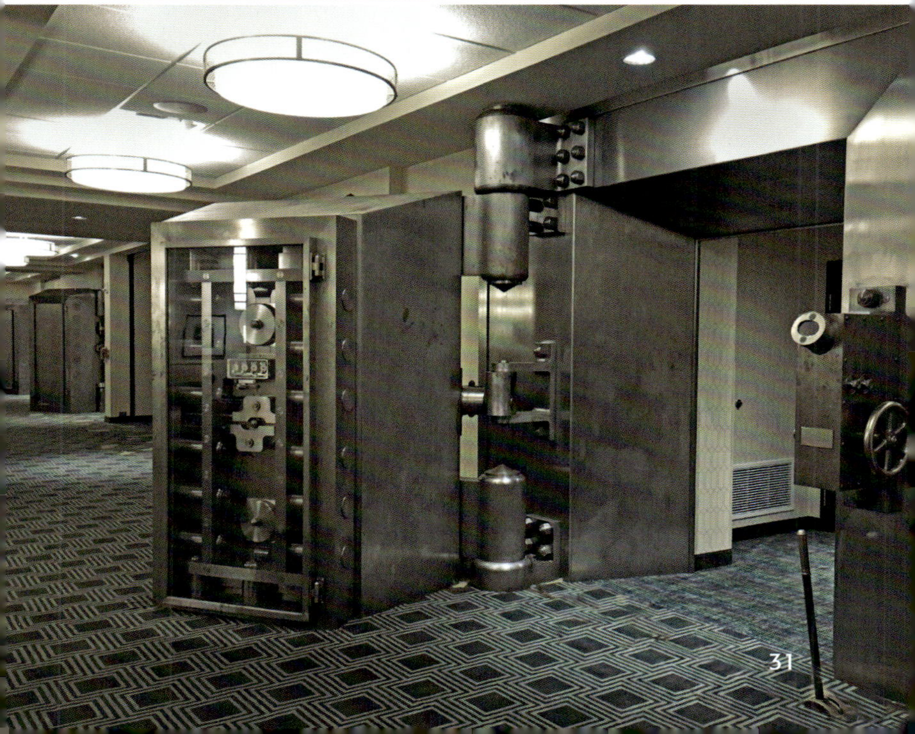

15. Gulf Tower*

*707 Grant Street
Trowbridge & Livingston (New York), architects;
E. P. Mellon, associate architect, 1930–32*

The Gulf Tower is to the right of the Koppers Building. The tops of both buildings are lighted at night.

This 44-story building, originally constructed for the Gulf Oil Corporation, was the tallest in Pittsburgh at 582 feet until 1970. The architects went down 90 feet to find a proper footing for their great tower, then raised it in a sober Modernistic manner that began and ended with allusions to Classical architecture: notice the stepped-back pyramidal top recalling the Mausoleum at Halicarnassus (353 B.C.), one of the seven wonders of the ancient world, and the colossal doorway on Seventh Avenue with its 50-ton granite entablature. For decades, the Gulf Building forecast the weather, using red and blue, solid and flashing neon lights. A newly designed KDKA Weather Beacon—using LED lights—debuted on July 4, 2012. The pyramidal top now forecasts the weather through color-coded signals and marks national holidays, sports moments, and other celebrations.

Cross Seventh Avenue. Enter the Koppers Building from Grant Street and walk through the opulent Art Deco lobby to William Penn Place.

16. Koppers Building*

*436 Seventh Avenue
Graham, Anderson, Probst & White (Chicago), architects, 1927–29*

The successor firm to D. H. Burnham & Company of Chicago designed a suave Art Deco headquarters for a progressive industrial firm (manufacturers of coke-derived byproducts).

Koppers Building interior

Art Deco, also known as Art Moderne, could adapt almost anything—traditional architectural styles such as Classical or Gothic, natural floral or water forms, and technological innovations like the automobile and the airplane—into characteristic exaggerated, elongated, geometrized, or streamlined patterns. The Koppers Building ornamentation is taken from nature: leaves and ferns are elegantly stylized.

The 34-story skyscraper is 475 feet high. The granite and limestone facing of the building, like the tall lobby spaces inside with their colored marbles and ornamented bronzework, suggests a cool urbanity remote from industrial toil.

The crowning chateau roof, being made of copper, can be taken as a pun on the corporate name, while the lobby mailbox is a doll's house version of the whole building, roof included.

Exit onto William Penn Place and walk south to Strawberry Way. You will pass the Alden & Harlow and Windrim sections of the Verizon Building (site 17).

17. Verizon Building

416 Seventh Avenue
Frederick J. Osterling, architect, 1890;
Alden & Harlow, architects for addition, 1905;
James T. Windrim (Philadelphia), architect for additions, 1915, 1923, 1931

Seventh Avenue

There are two distinct parts to the former Bell Telephone Building: Osterling's red-brick Romanesque (facing Seventh Avenue), and Alden & Harlow and Windrim's multi-phase annex (facing Seventh Avenue and William Penn Place and extending to Strawberry Way). Of the whole complex, what appears to be the last part is the best. A one-story covered walk on Strawberry Way, with shallow vaults in green-and-cream Guastavino tile and limestone piers, is not only an elegant space in itself but frames the view across the narrow street of three tiny houses c. 1850, a fragment of old Pittsburgh.

Either view Smithfield United Church (site 18) from a distance from William Penn Place and Strawberry Way, or walk west on Strawberry Way to Smithfield Street where the church is located. If the main doors are open, walk inside and up the stairs to the main sanctuary to see a series of stained glass windows by Ludwig Von Gerichten commemorating significant events in the life of the congregation and in Pittsburgh's history, including Abraham Lincoln's visit here in 1861.

18. Smithfield United Church*

620 Smithfield Street
Henry Hornbostel, architect, 1925–26

Here, Hornbostel designed a new church for a German Evangelical Protestant congregation of long existence, one of the recipients of land in 1787 from the heirs of William Penn. He finished off an eclectic Gothic Revival composition with an openwork spire that represents a very early architectural use of aluminum. The 80-foot spire was designed to be wholly of this material, but City officials did not trust the new metal and required that the frame be of steel though the panels are indeed of aluminum. A decorative banding at the base of the spire and an ornate cresting on the ridge of the main roof also are of aluminum.

Return to William Penn Place and Strawberry Way.
Continue south on William Penn Place to sites 19, 20, and 21.

Exploring Pittsburgh

19. Allegheny HYP Club
619 William Penn Place
1894; Edward B. Lee, architect for remodeling, 1930

Workers' houses were remodeled to provide a gracious courtyard and cozy interiors for what was originally the Harvard-Yale-Princeton Club. The club membership is now open to graduates from any college or university. The rose window of the Smithfield United Church (from the former church of 1875) makes an impressive backdrop ornament to this picturesque, retiring scene in the middle of the city.

20. The Residences at the Historic Alcoa Building*
611 William Penn Place
Harrison & Abramovitz (New York), architects, 1951–53
Strada, architects for renovation, 2012–16

Originally constructed for Alcoa (Aluminum Company of America), this corporate headquarters building was designed to show off every decorative and functional use of aluminum. It was the lightest tall office building ever built, with the world's first aluminum façade. Inside, pinkish marble walls contrasted with the aluminum staircases, light fixtures, elevators, mail chutes, and sculpture. The relatively small, rounded-corner windows were innovative. Sealed with inflatable rubber gaskets, they could be swung completely around and washed from the inside. They were intended to evoke the windows of modern jet aircraft, giving Alcoa employees, while seated at their desks and looking out their windows, the feeling of taxiing toward the runway!

In 1998, Alcoa constructed a new building on the North Shore along the Allegheny River and donated this building to serve as the headquarters for various nonprofit organizations serving southwestern Pennsylvania. In 2012, PMC Property Group of Philadelphia acquired what had become the Regional Enterprise Tower, and converted floors 14 through 31 from offices to apartments. Much of the original interior detailing survives, although the elegant, aluminum-and-glass entrance structure on Sixth Avenue now houses tenants' bicycles.

21. Mellon Square

James A. Mitchell for Mitchell & Ritchey, architects; Simonds & Simonds, landscape architects, 1953–55

The Mellon family donated a block of Downtown real estate in 1949 to create this public plaza with street-level retail and a six-story parking garage beneath. *Greater Pittsburgh* noted in 1955: "On a Labor Day week-end at his home, James Mitchell drew up the basic concept of a park and underground garage. His sketch … won approval of [R. K.] Mellon." Named for Richard Beatty Mellon and Andrew W. Mellon, and funded by the Andrew W. Mellon Educational and Charitable Trust, Richard King Mellon Foundation, and Sarah Mellon Scaife Foundation, Mellon Square was completed on October 18, 1955. Slightly more than an acre, the surface park is an oasis of fountains, terrazzo walks, granite benches, and many varieties of plants.

The Pittsburgh Parks Conservancy completed a $10 million restoration of Mellon Square in 2014.

Mellon Square is a fine architecture-viewing platform. Look toward Smithfield Street to see:

• the aluminum spire of Smithfield United Church (site 18);

Heinz 57 Center

Oliver Building

Park Building

525 William Penn Place

500 Smithfield

Kimpton Hotel Monaco Pittsburgh

- the cream-colored terra-cotta **Heinz 57 Center**, originally a department store (Starrett & Van Vleck, New York, 1914–15);
- the stone and terra-cotta **Henry W. Oliver Building*** (D. H. Burnham & Company, Chicago, 1907–10), named in memory of Pittsburgh industrialist Henry W. Oliver (1840–1904). In 2015, the Embassy Suites by Hilton opened in the top floors; and
- the **Park Building** (George B. Post, New York, 1896), with crouching figures of Atlas holding up its cornice.

Look toward Oliver Avenue to see:

- **525 William Penn Place** (Harrison & Abramovitz, New York, 1950–51). The sleek skyscraper of limestone-ribbon piers inset with chevron-patterned aluminum panels was originally the headquarters for U.S. Steel; it is now the Pittsburgh headquarters for Citizens Bank.
- **500 Smithfield**, originally designed for Mellon Bank (Trowbridge & Livingston, with E. P. Mellon, New York, 1923–24), whose magnificent interior was destroyed in 1999 for the short-lived Lord & Taylor department store that closed in 2004.

Look toward William Penn Place and Sixth Avenue to see:

- the **Kimpton Hotel Monaco Pittsburgh** (MacClure & Spahr, architects, 1902–03;

enlarged by Joseph F. Kuntz, architect, 1924; renovations by Strada, architects, 2012–15) occupying a Classically inspired building faced in stone that was originally the Philadelphia Company Building and later the James H. Reed Building.

From Mellon Square walk to the corner of Smithfield Street and Sixth Avenue. Walk west on Sixth Avenue to sites 22 through 29.

22. Trinity Cathedral *
*328 Sixth Avenue
Gordon W. Lloyd (Detroit), architect, 1870–72; Carpenter & Crocker, architects for parish house, 1906*

Despite a fire in 1967 and some rearrangement for liturgical reasons, the interior retains much of its mid-Victorian character. The ceiling is a ribbed wagon roof, a pointed arch in form, painted pale blue.

Trinity includes the earliest documented stained glass memorial windows in Pittsburgh—by Henry E. Sharp Studio of New York City, c. 1871—and nave windows by Nicholas Parrendo of Pittsburgh's Hunt Stained Glass Studios, 1968. The pulpit of 1922 is by New York architect Bertram Goodhue.

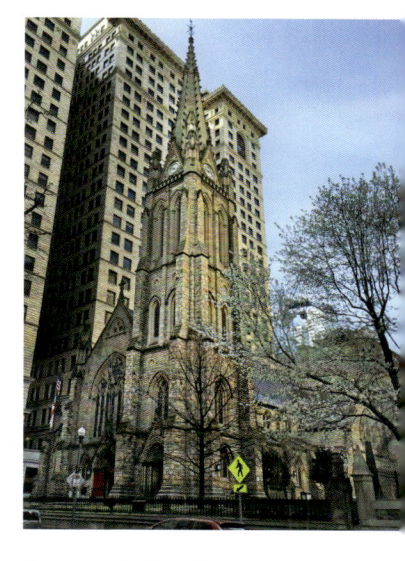

In honor of Pittsburgh's 250th anniversary in 2008, Trinity Cathedral completed a restoration campaign that included washing away more than 130 years of soot and grime from the sandstone exterior, restoring the rooster weathervane, rebuilding entrance steps and walkways, and restoring the burial ground containing some of the oldest graves in Pittsburgh.

23. First Presbyterian Church *
320 Sixth Avenue
Theophilus Parsons Chandler (Philadelphia), architect, 1903–05

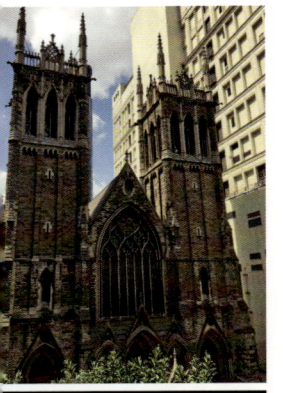

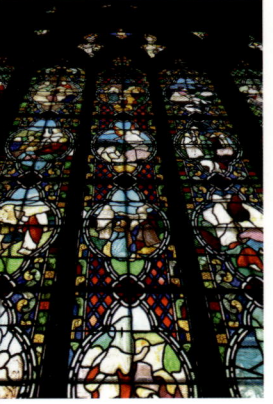

Like the neighboring Trinity Cathedral, this English Gothic Revival church—the congregation's fourth—stands on former property of the Penn family that was donated in 1787 for religious purposes.

Inside, the walls are made of small, rock-faced stones so that light breaks over them in a rippling texture. Arched trusses cased in heavily molded woodwork run the length of the nave, and enormous curved doors open effortlessly to reveal a chapel-like space with three tiers of Sunday school rooms on each side of a great south window *(see page 92)*.

The stained glass is notable. The south window—a genealogy of Christ—is by Clayton & Bell of London. One window in the nave is by Charles R. Lamb of New York. The other 13 nave windows by Frederick Wilson of Tiffany Studios were an experiment that the Tiffany firm never repeated. Slabs of rose-colored opalescent glass were painted with colored enamels in the 18th-century manner. The most famous window—the north window—is concealed, for the most part, by the organ. It was designed in 1904 by William Willet (1867–1921), who from 1897 to 1913 lived and worked in Pittsburgh with his wife and business partner, Anne Lee Willet. It is one of the most important American windows of its time for its attempt to revive medieval iconography.

Willet window, 1904–05

24. Duquesne Club

325 Sixth Avenue
Longfellow, Alden & Harlow, architects, 1887–89; Rutan & Russell, architects for addition to front right, 1902; Janssen & Cocken, architects for rear tower addition, 1930–31

Founded in 1873, the Duquesne Club is famous as a wealthy, conservative institution, traditionally the club of leading industrialists and businessmen. The architects for the 1887 design were a new firm, established in the previous year by MIT classmates Alexander Wadsworth Longfellow (1854–1934), Frank E. Alden (1859–1908), and Alfred B. Harlow (1857–1927). (Longfellow and Alden had worked under H. H. Richardson.) The firm originally had offices in both Boston and Pittsburgh, but business in both cities was so successful that the partners parted amicably in 1896; Longfellow took over the New England commissions, while Alden and Harlow remained in Pittsburgh.

The Duquesne Club is Richardsonian Romanesque with Classical elements, typical of these architects. The building has a simple dignity with gently textured brownstone walls and a balustrade emphasizing the roofline. The bay windows, typical of clubhouses in both Boston and London's West End, allow observation of the passing world from an elevated and rather private vantage point, which must have struck the clubmen as entirely right.

Exploring Pittsburgh

25. Granite Building

313 Sixth Avenue
Bickel & Brennan, architects, 1889–90; remodelings c. 1930, late 1980s

Former *New York Times* Style Editor Holly Brubach (a Pittsburgh native) is adapting the Richardsonian Romanesque Granite Building for new uses. The interior design of the eight-story building will combine 19th- and 21st-century details. Brubach's interest is in "imagining new lives for old buildings and in incorporating historic architecture in a contemporary cityscape, creating a conversation between the past and the present."

The building was originally constructed for the German National Bank, founded in 1860. Here, customers could transact business in German. The architects were Charles Bickel (1852–1921) and John P. Brennan (1857–1925), who designed many of Pittsburgh's fire and police stations. The firm dissolved around 1891; Brennan became an architect for the City, and Bickel, who designed the 1898 building for Kaufmann's Department Store (now Kaufmann's Grand on Fifth Avenue), maintained a successful practice until his death.

A bit of trivia: Oakmont Country Club was formed in this building, since club founder H. C. Fownes had his offices here. He and his associates met on August 17, 1903 to draw up papers of incorporation. In 1987, Oakmont Country Club became the first golf club and course to be designated a National Historic Landmark.

Plaques awarded by the Pittsburgh History & Landmarks Foundation identify more than 590 sites in the Pittsburgh region.

26. Wood Street Station and Wood Street Galleries *

*601 Wood Street
Edward Stotz, architect, 1927–28; renovated by IKM Incorporated, architects, and Parsons Brinckerhoff, engineers, 1984*

Edward Stotz (1868–1949) apprenticed with Andrew W. Peebles, Frederick J. Osterling, and others, and toured and sketched in Europe before establishing his own firm that continues today as MacLachlan, Cornelius & Filoni. He designed 903 structures in a 47-year career, including Church of the Epiphany (1902–03) in the Lower Hill, the Oakmont Clubhouse (1904), and the former Schenley High School (1915–16) in Schenley Farms.

Originally the Monongahela Bank, this triangular building on a triangular lot now houses an art gallery and the Wood Street Station, one of Downtown Pittsburgh's four "T" stations. Artwork in the station includes "Thirteen Geometric Figures," by Sol LeWitt; "Ornamental Frames," by Albert Paley; and "168 Light Bulbs," by Jim Campbell.

Two other light rail stations also opened in Downtown Pittsburgh in July 1985: Steel Plaza and Gateway Center. (However, that Gateway Center station was demolished in 2010 and a larger one was constructed across Liberty Avenue in 2009–12. Fortunately, African American artist Romare Bearden's ceramic mural of 1984, "Pittsburgh Recollections," was removed from the original station and reinstalled in the new station; *see pages 102–103*.) In 2002, the First Avenue Light Rail Transit Station opened, adjacent to PNC Firstside Center.

The Classical music played in the Downtown transit stations (and at Pittsburgh International Airport) is provided by WQED-FM and includes recordings of performances in Pittsburgh by Pittsburgh musicians.

Exploring Pittsburgh

27. Midtown Towers
643 Liberty Avenue
Thomas Hannah, architect, 1907

This eye-catching apartment tower, capped by a distinctive red dome, originally housed the offices of Colonel Thomas J. Keenan, chief owner of the *Penny Press* (founded in 1885 and later known as the *Pittsburgh Press*). At one time, Keenan was one of the largest landowners in the Triangle. He had an eye for publicity and erected an 18-story skyscraper decorated with portraits of 10 "worthies" associated with state and local history and politics. The fancy dome of fireproof poured-in-place concrete was once capped with the figure of an eagle in flight, and flags flew from the four smaller domes. Architect Thomas Hannah (1867–1935) probably modeled his design for the Keenan Building, as it was originally named, after the Spreckels Building of 1898 in San Francisco, later known as the Call Building.

Two of the ten portrait medallions: George Washington *(see page 74)* and Mary Croghan Schenley *(see page 75)*.

View the Cultural District from Liberty and Sixth avenues. Explore the places in entry 28 after this tour by attending a performance!

28. Cultural District

The Pittsburgh Cultural District, comprising 14 square-blocks, occupies land parallel to the Allegheny River between Stanwix and Tenth streets. It includes the Penn-Liberty National Register District and City Historic District. This grid of blocks was part of the original street plan of 1784 laid out by George Woods and Thomas Vickroy, who were commissioned by the heirs of William Penn to survey the family's private land holdings in Pittsburgh.

By 1900, the area was widely varied in content and fully built up. Commercial buildings large and small, theaters, hotels, office buildings, and some heavy industry were mixed together in that time before zoning. The ongoing century saw construction continuing until the Depression, then a half-century of deterioration.

A reversal of circumstances began in 1971 with the restoration and opening of **Heinz Hall** (the former Loew's Penn Theater designed in 1925–26 by Chicago architects Rapp & Rapp and renovated in 1970–71 by Stotz, Hess, MacLachlan & Fosner) for the Pittsburgh Symphony, and continued with the establishment of the Pittsburgh Cultural Trust in 1984.

Since then, the Trust has transformed a blighted section of the city into a world-class arts and entertainment district visited by over two million people each year. The **Benedum Center for the Performing Arts** (1926–27),

Benedum Center, 237 Seventh Street

Heinz Hall, 600 Penn Avenue

Katz Plaza, Penn Avenue and Seventh Street

Byham Theater (1903–04), and **Harris Theater** (c. 1931) are all in beautifully restored buildings. The Pittsburgh Public Theater's **O'Reilly Theater** (1999) and **Theater Square** (2003) were designed by architect Michael Graves (Princeton, NJ). Neighboring **Agnes R. Katz Plaza** (1999) contains a bronze fountain cascade 25 feet high and three pairs of benches in the form of eyes designed by sculptor Louise Bourgeois. Landscaping by Daniel Urban Kiley includes 32 linden trees.

Two hotels have opened in historic buildings in the Cultural District. The **Renaissance Pittsburgh Hotel,*** remodeled in 2001 by J. G. Johnson Architects (Denver), occupies the Fulton Building of 1905–06, designed by New York architect Grosvenor Atterbury. The **Courtyard Pittsburgh Downtown**, occupying 945-949 Penn Avenue (Phipps Pennsylvania Land Trust, Alfred C. Bossom, architect, New York, c. 1905–06), was renovated in 2004 by Perfido Weiskopf Architects.

The Cultural District also includes the **David L. Lawrence Convention Center**, designed in 2003 by Rafael Viñoly Associates PC (New York), and **Pittsburgh CAPA** (Creative

Byham Theater, 101 Sixth Street

Harris Theater, 809 Liberty Avenue

O'Reilly Theater, 621 Penn Avenue

Theater Square, 655 Penn Avenue

Renaissance Pittsburgh Hotel,
107 Sixth Street

Courtyard Pittsburgh Downtown,
945 Penn Avenue

David L. Lawrence Convention Center,
1000 Fort Duquesne Boulevard

Pittsburgh CAPA, 111 Ninth Street
(Charles Bickel's building at right)

Exploring Pittsburgh

and Performing Arts), a Pittsburgh Public School for grades 6–12, designed by MacLachlan, Cornelius & Filoni in 2003 and inspired, in part, by Charles Bickel's building of 1915, which was incorporated into CAPA.

Now called the August Wilson Center—African American Cultural Center, 980 Liberty Avenue

When Pittsburgh-born, Pulitzer-prize-winning playwright August Wilson died in 2005 during the planning of an African American arts center in the Cultural District, his widow, Constanza Romero, gave the center permission to honor his name. The **August Wilson Center for African American Culture,*** designed by African American architect Allison Williams for Perkins + Will (San Francisco Office), opened in 2009 and was LEED certified in 2012 *(see page 85)*. Go inside to see special exhibits, performances, and works by famed photographer Charles "Teenie" Harris (1908–98) and sculptor Thaddeus Mosley (b. 1926).

Walk back to Wood Street and Sixth Avenue to site 29.

29. 300 Sixth Avenue Building

528–542 Wood Street
D. H. Burnham & Company (Chicago), architects, 1902–04

McCreery & Company Department Store, established in 1850 in New York by Joseph McCreery, was the first tenant of the Wood Street Building, as it was originally called, commissioned by Henry W. Oliver and designed by D. H. Burnham & Company in 1902. McCreery & Company was the

authorized Western Pennsylvania agent for Gustav Stickley's Craftsman Workshop furniture, lighting fixtures, textiles, and accessories. Stickley was a leading proponent of American Arts and Crafts design, advertised throughout the country in his magazine, *The Craftsman*. Stickley products were displayed in a special "Craftsman's Room," and the dining rooms had Stickley furniture. Cuthbert P. Brangwyn (1875–1911), brother of English artist Frank Brangwyn, was head of interior design at McCreery & Company in Pittsburgh from 1906 to 1911. The Pittsburgh store closed in 1938.

The first three floors were refronted in brown marble in 1941–42. The mural of carved and colored glass was fabricated in 1939 by the Harriton Carved Glass Company (New York); it depicts a puddler stirring iron in a hot furnace as it changes into steel. The interior was remodeled for offices and a penthouse was added in the 1960s, where the Pittsburgh Press Club met.

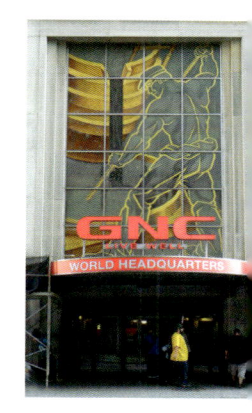

Walk south on Wood Street to sites 30 through 33.

30. Two PNC Plaza

620 Liberty Avenue (and Wood Street at Oliver Avenue) Skidmore, Owings & Merrill [SOM] (New York), architects, 1973–76

The senior SOM designers of these elegant Miesan towers, originally for Equibank, were Myron Goldsmith (1918–1996) and Natalie de Blois (1921–2013). De Blois joined SOM's New York office in 1944 and worked closely with Gordon Bunshaft until 1965 when she transferred to SOM's Chicago office; she resigned in 1974, the only woman to hitherto achieve Associate rank at SOM.

In 1973, senior partner Nathaniel Owings wrote: "[The firm] included just one woman: Natalie de Blois. Long, lean, quizzical, she seemed fit to handle all comers. Handsome, her dark, straight eyes invited no nonsense. Her mind and hands worked marvels in design—and only she and God would ever know just how many great solutions, with the imprimatur of one of the male heroes of SOM, owed much more to her than was attributed by either SOM or the client."

31. One PNC Plaza

249 Fifth Avenue
Welton Becket & Associates (Los Angeles), architects, 1967–71

The founder of the firm, Welton Becket (1902–1969), is best known for Los Angeles buildings such as the Los Angeles Music Center and Capital Records Tower Building. The Pittsburgh National Bank Building, now One PNC Plaza, is 30 stories. The first floor, once a public banking space, now houses a clothing store. The upper floors have columnless interiors, allowing for flexible office layouts. The exterior is granite.

Cross Fifth Avenue and continue walking south on the west side of Wood Street to see sites 32 and 33. Look up as you walk.

Downtown Walking Tour

32. The Tower at PNC Plaza
300 Fifth Avenue
Gensler (San Francisco), architects, 2011–15

In 2011, the design team for The Tower at PNC Plaza was challenged with an audacious goal: design the "greenest" high-rise in the world. In October 2015, this goal was achieved.

From a distance, the southeastern sloping roof with its solar chimney and the breathable glass skin with its thin, vertical, operable windows catch your eye; but from street-level, it's the colorful chandelier suspended from the lobby ceiling that becomes the focal point. Composed of 1,500 polycarbonate panels backed by LED lights, the "Beacon" *(below)* uses real-time data to visualize the performance of the 33-story corporate headquarters.

Designed to be the crown jewel of PNC's "green-building" efforts, the Tower exceeds LEED Platinum certification *(see page 85)*. Its most innovative, sustainable technology is its double-skin façade, a window system in which two panes of glass are separated by a cavity *(above)*. In natural ventilation mode, fresh air enters the cavity through the outer façade's operable windows, which automatically open and close depending on weather conditions, and then passes through the interior façade's vents. The fresh air travels across the office space and is exhausted through the Tower's solar chimney, which consists of two vertical shafts located at the building's core. The solar chimney and double-skin façade create a cyclical system in which fresh air enters the building, naturally warms, rises through the shafts, and exits at the roof.

A collaborative workplace for PNC Financial Services Group's 2,300 employees, the Tower includes three "green" roofs, an outdoor terrace on the third-floor *(see page 89)*, and a five-story, indoor, atrium park on the 28th floor. The glass façade of the indoor park is supported by 20 vertical cables. The park provides a breathtaking view south to Mt. Washington, and west over Market Square and Gateway Center to the Ohio River Valley.

Fifth Wood Building (corner) and 445, 443 and 439 Wood Street

33. 400 Block, Wood Street

Between 2012 and 2015, the Pittsburgh History & Landmarks Foundation (PHLF) restored six building façades on Wood Street (418, 420, 422; 419, 429, 445), as well as the Fifth Wood Building, "Skinny" Building *(see page 54)*, and two others nearby. Funding was provided by the state's Redevelopment Assistance Capital Program, under contract with and in partnership with the Urban Redevelopment Authority of Pittsburgh, through the Mayor's Downtown Preservation Program.

The **Fifth Wood Building** (Kashi Jewelers, 256 Fifth Avenue) was designed in 1922 by George H. Schwan. A red LED light band crowns its cornice, and accent lights enliven the façade at night. Kashi Jewelers also occupies the rare surviving wood-frame building from c. 1860 at **445 Wood Street**. The two adjacent buildings are worth noticing: **443 Wood Street** is a restrained Neo-Classical building of c. 1925 with a limestone façade, and **439 Wood Street** is a terra-cotta-clad building of c. 1910 with generously sized windows.

7-Eleven (right) and the "Skinny" Building at Forbes and Wood

For more than a century, the John M. Roberts & Son Company jewelry store occupied the elegant Neo-Classical building at **429–431 Wood Street**, designed in 1925 by local architect George M. Rowland. George Westinghouse, Diamond Jim Brady, singer Lillian Russell, and pianist Liberace were among their customers. Look up to see the restored bronze canopy and the cornice with lion heads and floral forms. 7-Eleven now occupies the storefront.

The block ends with the **"Skinny" Building** at 241 Forbes Avenue. At 5 feet 2 inches wide, this is one of the skinniest buildings anywhere. Built in 1926 to provide space for Louis Hendel to store fruit produce, this "Dollhouse Skyscraper" was adapted over the years for a lunch counter and beauty salon, and now houses an open-air clothing accessories shop.

Across Forbes Avenue, the handsome block of historic buildings continues on Wood Street. Since 1960, the Italian Sons and Daughters of America has owned **419 Wood Street**, designed in 1930 by Hunting, Davis & Dunnells. When

Downtown Walking Tour

Metal paneling was removed in 2012 from 419 Wood Street, revealing the original stonework and windows.

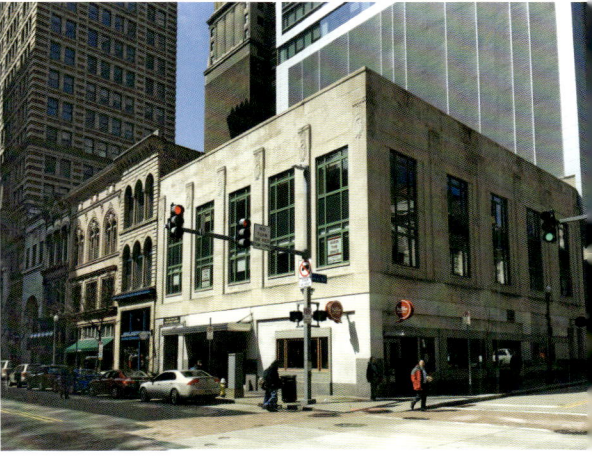

McDonald's became a tenant, the upper stories of the limestone building were covered with orange metal paneling and the windows were narrowed. PHLF removed the panels, filled 300 holes in the stone, and restored the windows. In 2011, PHLF and its subsidiary, Landmarks Development Corporation (LDC), acquired **413–417 Wood Street**. Work in subsequent

413 Wood Street, constructed in 1883 and refaced c. 1901, houses Peter Lawrence (green awning). Boutique La Passerelle is located next door, in a c.1875 building at 417 Wood Street.

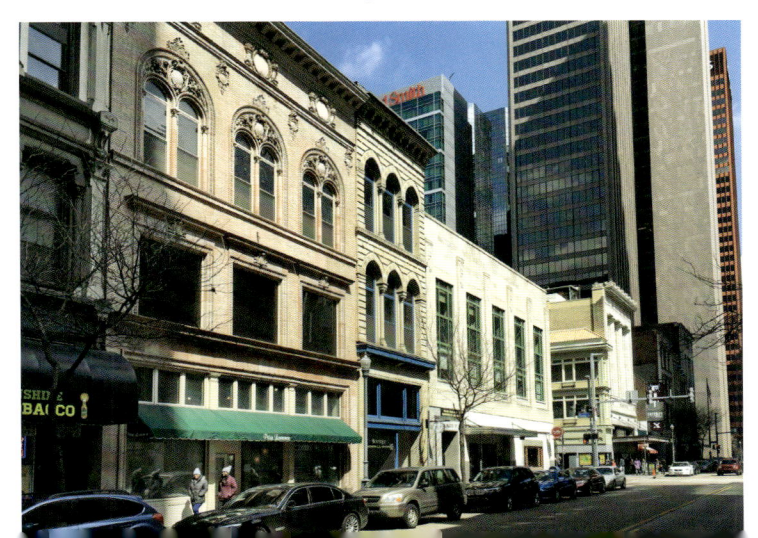

Exploring Pittsburgh

Three cast-iron buildings of c. 1875–1881, at 418–422 Wood Street, are shown before and after renovations in 2013.

years included restoring the stone façades and renovating the interiors for women's retail. PHLF also restored the three cast-iron façades across Wood Street at **418, 420,** and **422**, and LDC acquired 420 and 422. Concrete block, ceramic tile, and plaster were removed during the 15-month renovation. The missing or damaged cast-iron members were replaced with fiberglass facsimiles.

From Wood Street and Forbes look south on Wood to see site 34.

34. Point Park University Center

414 Wood Street
Frederick J. Osterling, architect, 1902, 1925–26; Sylvester Damianos, architect for remodeling, 1996

Point Park University, serving more than 4,500 students, is effectively combining new construction and historic preservation to enhance its campus along Wood Street, and including buildings on First Avenue, the Boulevard of the Allies, Fourth Avenue, and Forbes Avenue.

The University Center has entrances on three streets: Wood Street, Fourth Avenue, and Forbes Avenue. It was designed by Osterling for the Colonial Trust Company, a large financial institution. The façades on Fourth Avenue and Forbes Avenue were built in 1902 and the Wood Street entrance dates to 1925–26: notice the two fluted (grooved) Greek Ionic columns with scroll-like capitals.

As a result of a handsome renovation, the Point Park University Center houses a library, television studio, classrooms, and the GRW Theater, all within the T-shaped structure. The original skylit interior is framed in columns of Pavonazzo marble, and the bank vault has been transformed into a reading lounge. Students are able to enter the new Pittsburgh Playhouse from the University Center, and a marble staircase has been reopened.

At Wood Street and Forbes walk west on Forbes to sites 35, 36, and 37.

35. CVS/pharmacy

239 Forbes Avenue
William E. Snaman, architect, 1922

Originally this was Donahoe's Market and Cafeteria, a popular Pittsburgh grocer from 1923 to 1970. Notice the "D" above the second-floor windows, the Neo-Classical panels of fruits and vegetables, and the elegant urns in the window pediments. This 126-foot-long façade of white terra cotta is further distinguished by seven colossal Corinthian columns: the capitals are ornamented with acanthus leaves.

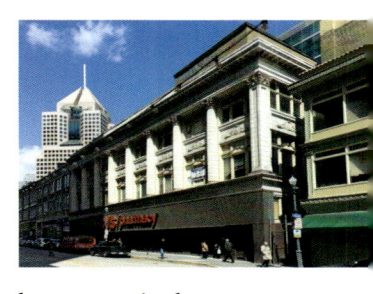

36. Market Square Place
Forbes Avenue, McMasters Way, and Fifth Avenue
Strada, architect for renovation and restoration, 2006–09

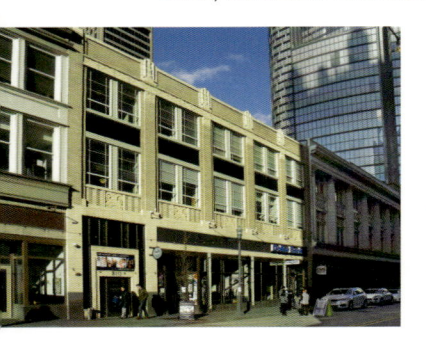

Although the address for Market Square Place is 222 Fifth Avenue, on this walking tour we see the Forbes Avenue façade first. The former G. C. Murphy Company Building (219 Forbes Avenue) and six adjacent historic buildings fronting on McMasters Way and Fifth Avenue were renovated by Downtown Streets Pittsburgh LP, a development team headed by Millcraft Industries, Inc., of Washington, Pennsylvania. The result is Market Square Place, a mixed-use development that initially included the YMCA of Greater Pittsburgh, 46 loft apartments, basement parking, and retail and restaurants. The developers used the federal 20 percent rehabilitation tax credit and received LEED Gold certification (*see page 85*). Market Square Place, Market at Fifth, Three PNC Plaza, and the Buhl Building (*see pages 63–65*) were among the first developments to revitalize the Market Square area.

The Art Deco building at 219 Forbes Avenue—note the "frozen fountains" jetting upwards and the stylized ferns and flowers—was designed in 1930 by H. E. Crosby (1899–1958), corporate architect of the G. C. Murphy Company, at a cost of $250,000. In 1906, George C. Murphy founded Murphy's 5 and 10 cents stores in McKeesport, 12 miles southeast of Pittsburgh. By the 1930s, there were 170 stores in 11 states. Even during the Great Depression 40 new stores were built.

Above: The award-winning Market Square Place borders Market Square at McMasters Way. Below: On Fifth Avenue, Market Square Place includes five historic building façades, from the red-brick corner building to the former Exchange National Bank Building (with flag), designed in 1922 by Weary & Alford (Chicago).

Exploring Pittsburgh

Above: Market Square, or the "Diamond," with the first Allegheny County Courthouse and market stalls, painted from memory after the Courthouse was demolished in 1852. The Courthouse occupied the western half of the Diamond and faced Market Street. Below: The Diamond Market, designed by Rutan & Russell, occupied Market Square from 1915 until 1961. This view is looking east toward Grant Street. Forbes (or Diamond) Street cut through the building from west to east, and Market Street cut through from south to north. The Diamond Market included a roller skating rink on the second floor.

The Graeme Street entrance to Market Square, with restaurants, coffee shops, and PPG Place.

37. Market Square

Market Square was laid out in 1784 when the Penn family had their property adjacent to Fort Pitt surveyed. The Penns gave this square to Pittsburgh to be used for public purposes. Like many public squares, it was called the "Diamond" because of the shape of the square when oriented to North on a compass. The corner where Graeme Street comes into Market Square marks the north point.

In the mid-1790s, Market Square became the site of the first Allegheny County Courthouse and neighboring market stalls; later a market house and City Hall occupied the square; and finally came the Diamond Market, a remarkable pair of buildings bridging Market Street and permitting Forbes Avenue to continue its passage. Since 1961, Market Square has remained open, a place for temporary art installations, a summer farmer's market, and other activities. In 2011, Klavon Design Associates completed the most recent redesign of Market Square.

Notable buildings surrounding the square include the

Exploring Pittsburgh

Original Oyster House of 1870, anchoring the northeast corner, where oysters once sold for a penny and beer was 10 cents a glass. To the southeast is **Primanti Brothers**, occupying the corner building in a handsome block of vernacular buildings constructed soon after Pittsburgh's Great Fire of 1845. To the southwest, one wing of **PPG Place** (*see page 70*) fronts on Market Square. Walter C. Kidney suggested that the black and silver uniform upright elements of PPG Place looked "like a Prussian regiment formed up to impress the peasants."

Look northward to see **EQT Plaza** (Kohn Pedersen Fox, New York, 1984–87), a 32-story skyscraper flanked by two arched-roof trusses in the form of a bridge, and **Fifth Avenue Place** (Hugh Stubbins Associates, Boston, 1985–87, with Williams Trebilcock Whitehead), with its distinctive mast.

Follow Market Street north to Fifth Avenue.

Highmark is the major tenant in Fifth Avenue Place (left). EQT Plaza (right) was first called CNG Tower and then Dominion Tower.

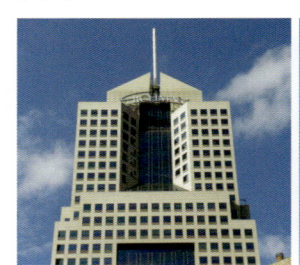

38. Market at Fifth

*Fifth Avenue between Market Street and Graeme Street
C. 1870 (architect/builder unknown); Alden & Harlow, architects, 1908–09; Janssen & Abbott, architects, 1907 (remodeled after 1926, architect unknown)
Landmarks Design Associates, architects for remodeling, 2007–09*

Market at Fifth, developed through a limited partnership of Landmarks Development Corporation, a subsidiary of the Pittsburgh History & Landmarks Foundation (PHLF), successfully used the federal 20 percent rehabilitation tax credit and achieved LEED Gold certification (*see page 85*). Three historic buildings—two from the 1870s and one from 1908—have been rescued, restored, and adapted to house seven apartments and two retail tenants: **Heinz Healey's Gentlemen's Apparel** and **Nettleton Shoe Shop**. A fourth building, the former John R. Thompsons Building at 435 Market Street (a 1907 commercial building designed by Janssen & Abbott and refaced in the late 1920s or 1930s), has been handsomely restored as the **Market Street Grocery**.

The City owned the 1908 building and two 1870s buildings and allowed them to deteriorate. They were slated for demolition in 1999 under Mayor Tom Murphy's plan to clear more than 60 buildings in the area of Fifth and Forbes avenues.

This plan was defeated in 2001 after vigorous opposition from PHLF, community stakeholders, and the National Trust for Historic Preservation.

The 1908 Arts & Crafts building facing Fifth Avenue, with its deep overhanging roof, wooden window framing and stucco, is the most architecturally significant of the group. It was designed for the Regal Shoe Company by Alden & Harlow, the city's leading architectural firm between 1896 and 1908. The two brick buildings fronting on Market and Graeme streets were constructed c. 1870 in the Italianate style, with overhanging eaves, a bracketed-cornice, and cast-iron window hoods.

A complex, award-winning restoration, Market at Fifth led the way in bringing locally owned quality retail and middle-income housing back to Fifth Avenue.

Cross Fifth Avenue at Market Street. Look back to see site 39.

39. Buhl Building

204 Fifth Avenue
Janssen & Abbott, 1913

Real estate developer Franklin Nicola commissioned this building and named it the Bash Building for his principal tenant; in 1922, however, Henry Buhl purchased and renamed the building. Architectural historian Walter C. Kidney described this as "a little gem of a building, clad in blue- and creamy-white terra cotta thickly decorated with Renaissance motifs"—urns on pedestals festooned with wreaths and ribbons. Janssen & Abbott's 1912–13 monochromatic addition to Kaufmann's Department Store may be considered a subdued sibling. In 2010, N & P Properties, owner of the Buhl Building, tastefully remodeled the first floor and agreed to donate a preservation easement to the Pittsburgh History & Landmarks Foundation to protect the exterior in perpetuity.

40. Three PNC Plaza* and PNC Triangle Park
201 Fifth Avenue
Gensler (San Francisco) with Astorino, 2006–10
LaQuatra Bonci Associates, landscape architects, 2009

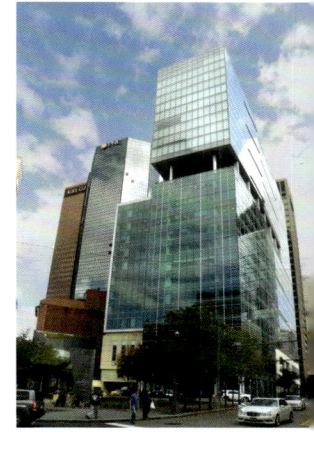

Pittsburgh's first new high-rise since the 1980s, Three PNC Plaza was one of the nation's largest, mixed-used, "green" buildings when it opened in 2009 (*see page 85*). The 23-story building includes PNC and the law firm Reed Smith; the Fairmont Pittsburgh with 185 guest rooms and a health club; 28 condominiums in the upper stories; and a restaurant, retail space, and underground parking. Go inside to see a small but significant display of artifacts, some of the 25,000 discovered during excavations beneath the Fifth Avenue site. PNC contracted with the Pittsburgh History & Landmarks Foundation to oversee the archeological excavation.

Cross Market Street to enter PNC Triangle Park. (Look across Liberty Avenue to see Heinz Hall Plaza.) From the park, cross Fifth Avenue and walk south on Graeme Street into Market Square. Continue south through Market Square to Fourth Avenue. Walk east to site 41.

41. Burke's Building
209 Fourth Avenue
John Chislett, architect, 1836; Landmarks Design Associates and Robert J. Kobet, AIA, architects for renovation, 1997

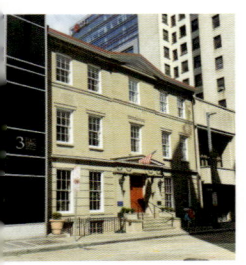

In contrast to the mirrored surface of PPG Place (*see page 70*) is the sandstone façade of what was originally the Burke's Building—the oldest work of high-style architecture in the city. John Chislett (1800–1869), English-born and trained, designed Pittsburgh's first office building in the Greek Revival style. It survived the Great Fire of 1845. In 1996–97, the Burke's Building was among the first in Pittsburgh to be renovated according to "green" energy-conservation principles when it was adapted to house the Western Pennsylvania Conservancy. Now privately owned, the façade of the office building is protected in perpetuity from alteration through an easement with the Pittsburgh History & Landmarks Foundation (PHLF).

From the Burke's Building, look east on Fourth Avenue to see some of the buildings included in site 42. Or, walk along Fourth Avenue to Smithfield Street to see all the buildings. Then return to PPG Place, site 43.

42. Fourth Avenue Historic District

Once Pittsburgh's "Wall Street"—complete with a stock exchange and 108 chartered banks and trust companies—Fourth Avenue is one of 18 National Register Historic Districts in the city. A view from PPG Place shows five buildings of similar height, showing different approaches to the compositional challenge posed by the skyscraper in the early 1900s.

- The **Benedum-Trees Building*** of 1905 (Thomas H. Scott, 1865–1940) is a transitional tall building with heavy detailing and two massive cornices at the top. And yet, white brick and white terra cotta,

Downtown Walking Tour

readily cleaned, show a new attitude to Downtown architecture.

- In the **Investment Building** of 1927 (John M. Donn, Washington, D.C.), a darker and more textured brown brick is in fashion. There is a simplicity and lightness of form and detailing. Limestone obelisks accent the skyscraper's top corners.

- The **Arrott Building** * of 1901–02 (Frederick J. Osterling) shows the desire of the turn-of-the-century architect to decorate all parts of a building; note the balconies, bands of white terra cotta and golden-orange brick, and massive cornice and crowning cheneau. Ornamental bronze and heavily veined marble inlaid with Cosmati mosaic borders adorn the tall, narrow lobby that is full of character. In 2018, work began on converting the former office building into a boutique hotel.

- The **Bank Tower**,* originally the Peoples Savings Bank Building (Alden & Harlow, 1901–02), is rusticated (deeply grooved) at its base, and then rises in a heavily ornamented deep-red-brick and terra-cotta shaft.

- Across the street is the former Union National Bank of 1906 (MacClure & Spahr), an elegantly simple design of gray granite with a rounded-corner entrance. Now **The Carlyle**, the building houses 60 condominiums. Its façade will be preserved in perpetuity, thanks to an easement donation to PHLF.

Beyond Wood Street, the historic Fourth

Top to bottom: **Investment Building, Arrott Building, Bank Tower,** and **The Carlyle.**

Exploring Pittsburgh

Avenue financial district continues east to Smithfield Street. Notable buildings include:

- the former **Commonwealth Trust Company** of 1906 (Frederick J. Osterling), with colossal Ionic columns. The 20-story building is being renovated for residences.
- the Richardsonian Romanesque **Times Building** of 1892 (Frederick J. Osterling), built for the *Pittsburgh Times* newspaper. The building now houses a post office, offices, and a restaurant.
- the former Industrial Bank of 1903 (Charles M. Bartberger), a small but impressive building with a great entrance arch. The Pittsburgh Stock Exchange was housed there from 1962 to 1974. Point Park University acquired the building, restored the stained-glass ceiling, and incorporated the historic structure into the **Pittsburgh Playhouse**.
- the **Pittsburgh Engineers' Building**, originally the Union Trust Company building of 1898. It was the first Pittsburgh work of D. H. Burnham & Company, a Chicago architectural firm. Notice the cool and correct Grecian Doric temple front—with the plain, cushion-shaped column capitals—and the big, florid acroteria on the triangular pediment. This is now the headquarters of the Engineers' Society of Western Pennsylvania. An interior vault is used as a dining space.

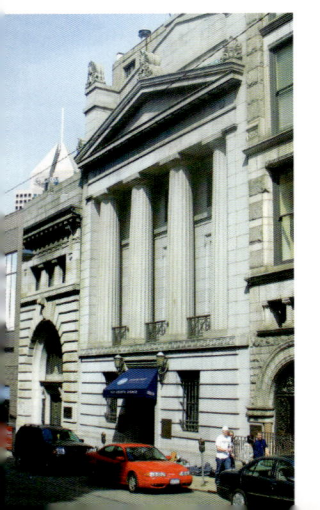

Left: The former Industrial Bank/Pittsburgh Playhouse (arched entrance) and the Engineers' Building (blue canopy).

Commonwealth Trust Company Building

Times Building

Downtown Walking Tour

- the **Standard Life Building**, originally the Pittsburgh Bank for Savings, a work of 1903 by Alden & Harlow. Sporting dark stonework and exuberant Classical detailing, the early skyscraper is reminiscent of an Italian Renaissance palazzo. The upper stories of the building have been converted into housing.

Standard Life Building (right)

- the brownstone **Dollar Bank**,* designed in 1870 by Philadelphia architect Isaac Hobbs and enlarged in 1906 by James T. Steen. Go inside to see the best preserved early 20th-century banking space in Downtown Pittsburgh and an impressive Heritage Center.

Retrace your steps on Fourth Avenue to PPG Place.

Dollar Bank

Looking east on Fourth Avenue (below).

69

43. PPG Place

Johnson/Burgee Architects (New York), 1979–84

PPG Place is the headquarters of PPG Industries (formerly Pittsburgh Plate Glass Company). The 40-story mirrored-glass Post-Modern tower is surrounded by five ancillary buildings capped by 231 pinnacles. In the words of Philip Johnson (1906–2005): "The tower idea came from the Cathedral of Learning, the famous Gothic Tower of the University of Pittsburgh. The idea of the series of towers came from Richardson's Allegheny County Courthouse. … it's a village idea. A cathedral and the low buildings around its base make a square." Johnson designed the obelisk to be the sole object in the granite-paved square. Pittsburghers, though, felt the austere square needed more. Thanks to a gift from the Hillman Foundation in 2001–02, a fountain enlivens the square in the summer and an ice rink is installed each winter.

From PPG Place, walk west to Stanwix Street. Cross Stanwix to see sites 44 and 45.

44. St. Mary of Mercy Church

202 Stanwix Street
William P. Hutchins, architect, 1936

William P. Hutchins (1883–1941), born in Wales and educated in Pittsburgh, was an important Pittsburgh Roman Catholic designer of churches, schools, and convents. Here, he erected two red brick walls at the property line, cutting deep, lancet-arched window openings into them. The corner tower is kept low, with a simple, strong shape, so the church maintains its dignity in the Downtown area. The vivid red brick complements the silver reflective glass of PPG Place.

To the left of the church entrance, about five feet up, is a plaque indicating the 46-foot "All-time-high water mark" of the St. Patrick's Day Flood that crested on March 18, 1936. The disaster spurred flood-control development on Pittsburgh's three rivers.

45. Four Gateway Center

444 Liberty Avenue
Max Abramovitz of Harrison & Abramovitz
(New York), architect, 1958–60

This is the most elegant exterior of any of Max Abramovitz' Pittsburgh buildings. The structure of the building—the stainless steel mullions—is dramatically displayed on the outside of the skyscraper and a continuous curtain wall of glass hangs behind. The tall, windowless shaft contains the service core of elevators, stairs, and restrooms. Walk up the stairs and stroll through the rooftop garden plaza (above an underground garage), designed in 1961 by Schell & Deeter, with Simonds & Simonds, landscape architects.

Exploring Pittsburgh

From Stanwix Street walk north to Liberty Avenue. Turn west on Liberty and walk to see the last three sites: 46, 47, and 48.

46. Gateway Center One, Two, and Three
401 Liberty Avenue
Eggers & Higgins (New York), architects, with Irwin Clavan, 1950–53; Clarke + Rapuano (New York), landscape architects

Built with a major post-war investment of the Equitable Life Assurance Society, Gateway Center One, Two, and Three were the first buildings of Pittsburgh's Renaissance. This was the first publicly sponsored, privately financed urban redevelopment project in the United States. Blocks of privately owned buildings, including warehouses, were demolished and replaced with three gleaming cruciform office towers, clad in stainless steel and set on a landscaped pedestrian plaza with underground parking. The repetitive cruciform towers recall Le Corbusier's unrealized scheme of 1922 for rebuilding the city of Paris. The result, according to some critics, was not distinguished; as early as 1961, authors John Burchard and Albert Bush-Brown cited Gateway Center as an example of the "failure" of architects (and their clients) in the 1950s to create livable and attractive urban spaces. Roberta Brandes Gratz confirmed this opinion 30 years later in *The Living City: How America's Cities Are Being Revitalized*. Patricia Lowry, architecture critic of the *Pittsburgh Post-Gazette*, summed up the impact of Gateway Center: "Ninety buildings came down [some of great architectural distinction] to realize the towers-in-a-park dream of Gateway Center, which, along with smoke and flood control, gave the city's image a big boost. But without first-floor retail, the plan ultimately contributed to downtown's decline as a shopping center."

47. Wyndham Grand Pittsburgh Downtown

600 Commonwealth Place
William B. Tabler, Jr., architect (for Hilton hotels), 1957–59;
Stephen Berry (Youngstown, OH), architect for addition and renovations, 2007–14

When this hotel was first proposed in 1954 during Pittsburgh's Renaissance, one idea discussed was to replace Richardson's Allegheny County Jail with the modern hotel. Preservationists opposed the idea and Conrad Hilton instead acquired this site for his hotel, with excellent views of Point State Park and the three rivers. The upper floors of the hotel are sheathed in panels of gold-anodized aluminum (now painted), and most of the guest rooms have floor-to-ceiling windows. It became the Wyndham Grand in 2010.

48. Point State Park

601 Commonwealth Place
Ralph E. Griswold, landscape architect, and Charles Morse Stotz, architect, 1945–74;
Pressley Associates, Inc. (Cambridge, MA), landscape architects for renovation, 2001–13

Here, on the smoldering ruins of the abandoned French Fort Duquesne (1754–58), British General John Forbes arrived on November 25, 1758 to claim this land for Great Britain. Forbes named Pittsburgh in honor of Sir William Pitt the Elder, the British statesman who devised the military strategy whereby Great Britain defeated France in Western Pennsylvania (during

Looking west to Point State Park and the three rivers (from left): Monongahela, Ohio, and Allegheny.

the French and Indian War) and around the world (during the Seven Years War). George Washington was the commander of the Virginia Regiment with the successful Forbes campaign. He was here when Pittsburgh was founded and named. Washington had, in fact, explored this land at the "Forks of the Ohio" five years earlier, in 1753, and had recommended then that the British build a fort here. When Fort Pitt was completed in 1761, it was one of the largest military fortifications in North America. Fort Pitt withstood one Indian siege in 1763. By 1772, the British sought to reduce their presence on the frontier, so they sold Fort Pitt to land speculators William Thompson and Alexander Ross. American forces used the fort during the Revolutionary War and finally abandoned it in 1792. Eventually, almost all of the fort was dismantled as the frontier town grew in its place.

Downtown Walking Tour

The Fort Pitt Museum and Fort Pitt Block House in Point State Park.

In the 1950s, acres of railroad yards and warehouses were cleared during Pittsburgh's Renaissance. The "Forks of the Ohio" was designated a National Historic Landmark in 1960 and the 36-acre Point State Park, straddled by an interstate highway, was completed in 1974. Ralph Griswold's landscape design for the park included only trees and plants native to the region in the 1750s. Beginning in 2001, Riverlife, a private nonprofit, initiated a master-planning process and secured funding for and supervised an extensive renovation of the park.

In Point State Park, visit the **Fort Pitt Museum,*** opened in 1969 in a reconstructed bastion, and the original **Fort Pitt Block House,*** a redoubt of 1764 constructed by British Colonel Henry Bouquet. The Block House is the oldest building in the City of Pittsburgh. No shot was ever fired from the Block House in defense. In time, it was converted into a trading post, a private residence, and eventually a tenement. Mary Croghan Schenley inherited the Block House from her grandfather, James O'Hara, and in 1894 gifted it to the Daughters of the American Revolution for preservation. Since 1895, the Block House has been open to the public as a museum.

You can also walk along the outline of Fort Duquesne and, during most months of the year, see the 150-foot-high fountain. After 260 years of growth and change, the Point remains the historical and symbolic heart of the Pittsburgh region.

Exploring Pittsburgh

Downtown Walking Tour

The Portal Bridge (1961–63), connecting the Fort Pitt Bridge (over the Monongahela River) and the Fort Duquesne Bridge (over the Allegheny River), was carefully designed to create an inviting entryway into Point State Park and to support an interstate highway. Suggested by Gordon Bunshaft, an architect with Skidmore, Owings & Merrill, and designed by architects Charles and Edward Stotz and engineer George S. Richardson, the Portal Bridge spans 182 feet and rises just 23 feet above the ground with a crest less than three feet from the road deck. To make the arch's shallow proportions possible, tightly stretched steel-wire tendons were anchored into the abutments and embedded in the concrete. The bridge's post-tensioning system was designed by French engineer Eugène Freyssinet.

Liverpool Street, Manchester

South Side Slopes and Flats

A Final Note

Adapted from Pittsburgh in Your Pocket: A Guide to Pittsburgh-area Architecture, *by Walter C. Kidney (PHLF, 1988)*

This is necessarily a brief sampling of the local architecture and landscape. Let us add a word of general advice. Walk around the Golden Triangle, particularly on a weekday when you can get into office building lobbies. Walk over an Allegheny River bridge to explore the North Side's historic neighborhoods of Deutschtown, the Mexican War Streets, Allegheny West, and Manchester. Cross the Smithfield Street Bridge to explore Station Square and the South Side Flats. If your car is in good heart, try some of the more dramatic hillside streets on the slopes. Walk in Oakland between Schenley Park and the residential area of Schenley Farms. Drive around Shadyside, Point Breeze, and Squirrel Hill. Drive along the rivers, and consult your instinct about exploring inland. You will be pleasantly surprised to discover many architectural landmarks set against an often dramatic terrain.

A portion of the Three Rivers Heritage Trail is part of the Great Allegheny Passage bike trail.

For more information about the architectural heritage of the Pittsburgh region, see page 91 for a listing of publications and self-guided walking tour pamphlets. To comment on this guidebook, contact: **info@phlf.org.**

Thompson's

Appendix

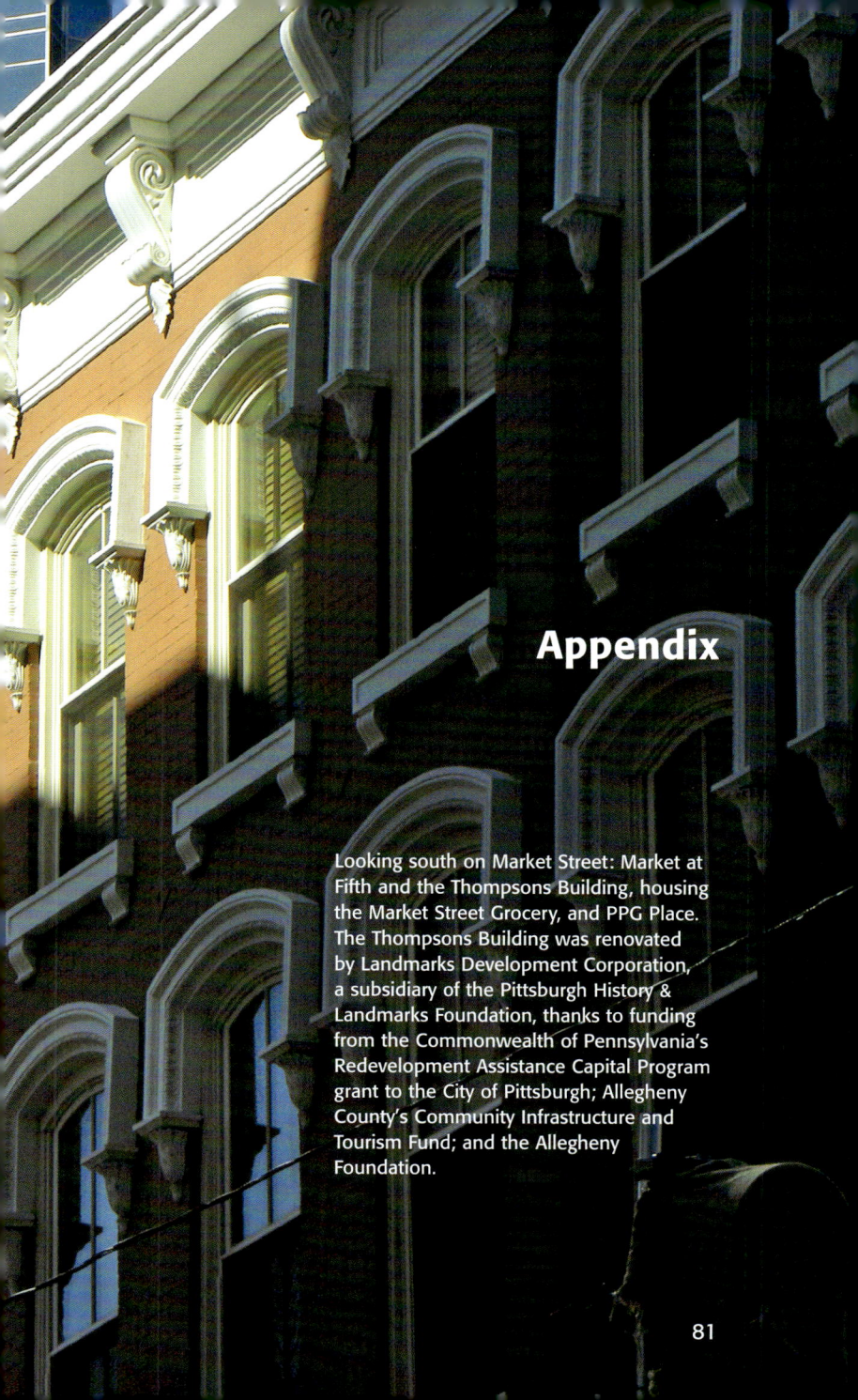

Looking south on Market Street: Market at Fifth and the Thompsons Building, housing the Market Street Grocery, and PPG Place. The Thompsons Building was renovated by Landmarks Development Corporation, a subsidiary of the Pittsburgh History & Landmarks Foundation, thanks to funding from the Commonwealth of Pennsylvania's Redevelopment Assistance Capital Program grant to the City of Pittsburgh; Allegheny County's Community Infrastructure and Tourism Fund; and the Allegheny Foundation.

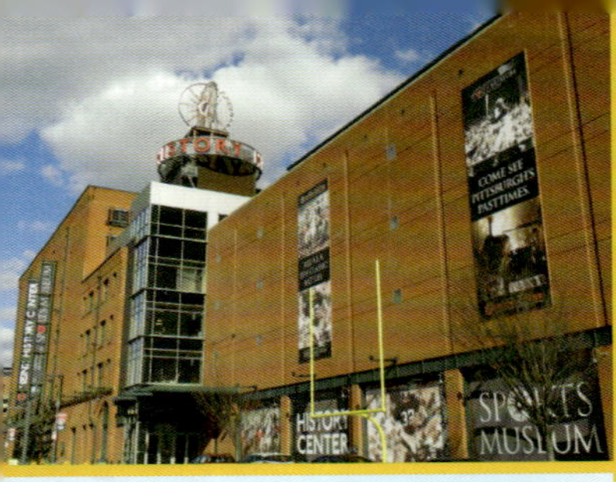
HISTORY CENTER
SPORTS MUSEUM
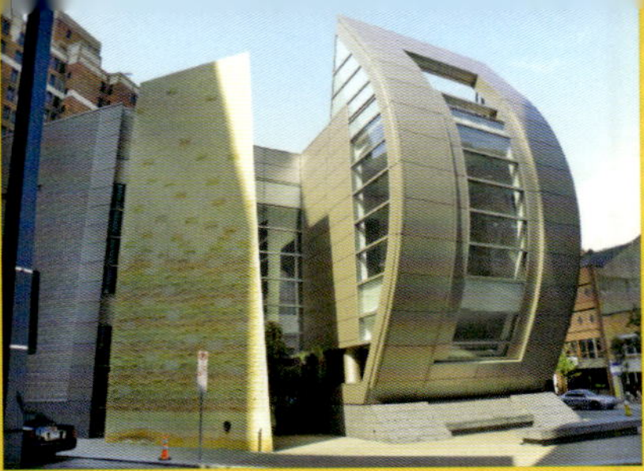
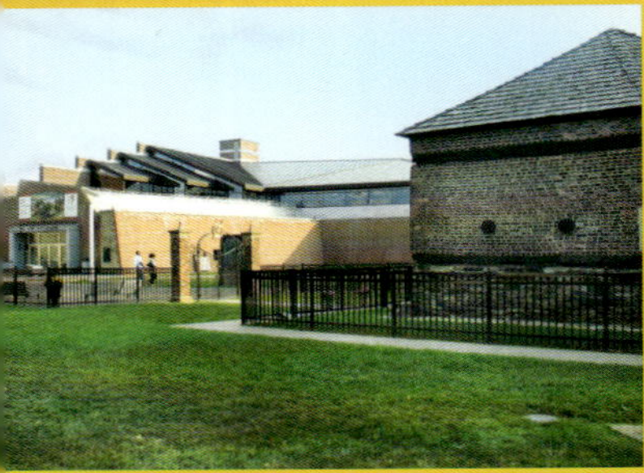
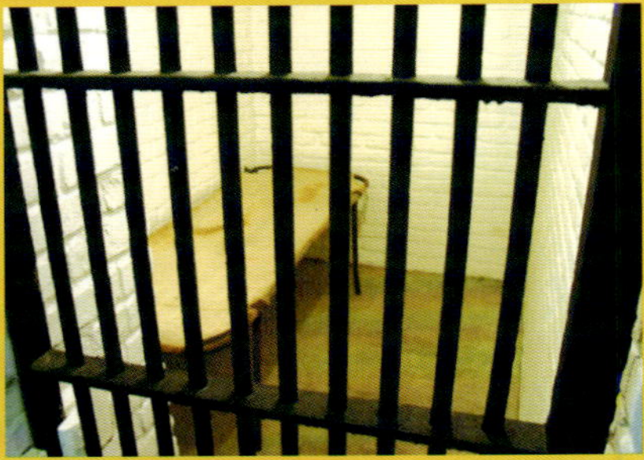
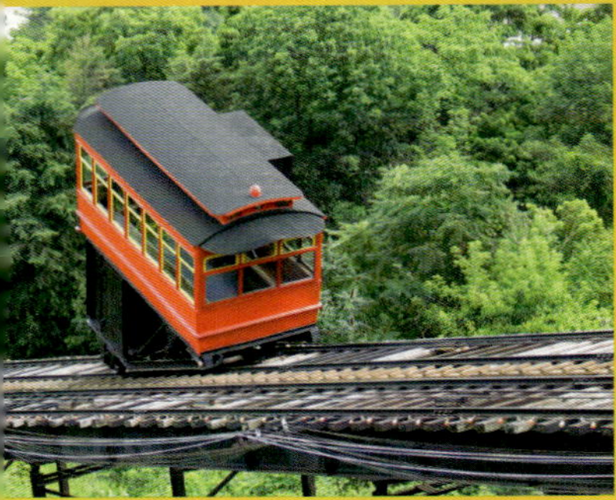
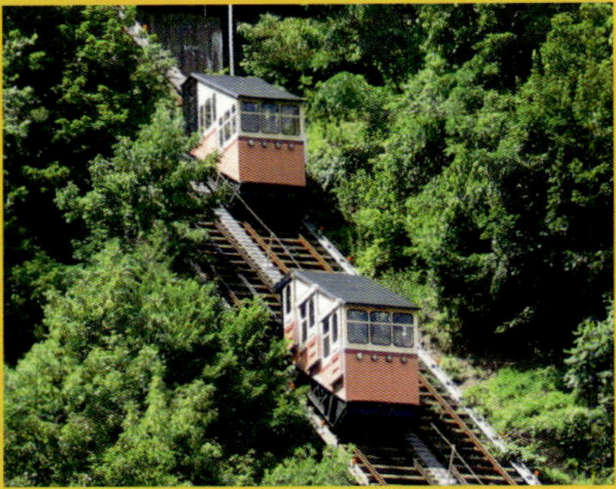
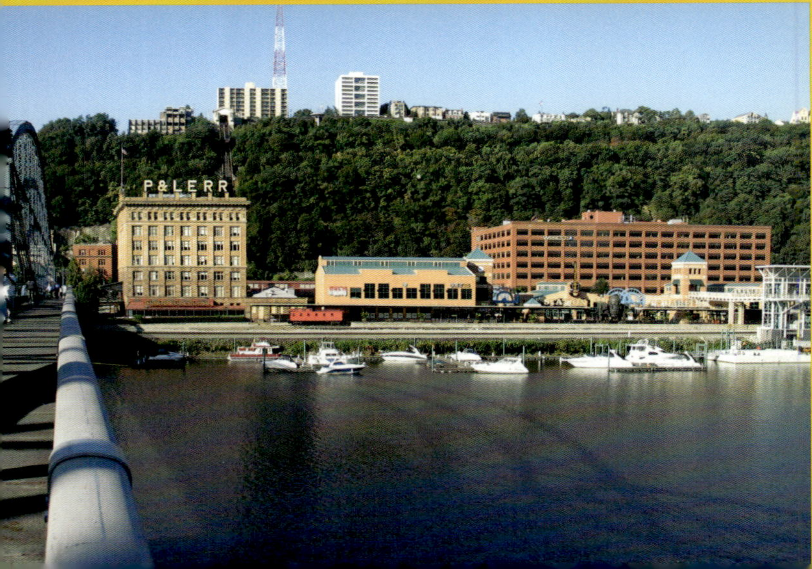
P&LERR

Downtown Museums and More

Senator John Heinz History Center
Western Pennsylvania Sports Museum
1212 Smallman Street, Pittsburgh, PA 15222
412-454-6000   www.heinzhistorycenter.org

August Wilson Center—African American Cultural Center
(see page 48)
980 Liberty Avenue, Pittsburgh, PA 15222
412-339-1011   www.AACC-AWC.org

Fort Pitt Museum *(see page 75)*
601 Commonwealth Place, Pittsburgh, PA 15222
412-281-9284   www.heinzhistorycenter.org
An affiliate of the Senator John Heinz History Center

Fort Pitt Block House *(see page 75)*
601 Commonwealth Place, Pittsburgh, PA 15222
412-471-1764   www.fortpittblockhouse.com

Allegheny County Jail Museum *(see page 13)*
(Allegheny County Court of Common Pleas, Family Division)
400 Ross Street, Pittsburgh, PA 15219
For Jail Museum information: 412-471-5808   www.phlf.org

Duquesne Incline
1197 West Carson Street, Pittsburgh, PA 15219 or
1220 Grandview Avenue, Pittsburgh, PA 15211
412-381-1665   www.duquesneincline.org

Monongahela Incline
2 Grandview Avenue, Pittsburgh, PA 15211
412-442-2000   www.portauthority.org
(Enter "Monongahela Incline" in search box)

Station Square
125 West Station Square Drive, Pittsburgh, PA 15219
412-261-2811   www.stationsquare.com

Other major attractions within a brisk 30-minute walk from Downtown Pittsburgh include the Andy Warhol Museum, Carnegie Science Center, Children's Museum Pittsburgh, National Aviary, Allegheny Commons, and Mattress Factory—all on the North Side—and South Side's historic East Carson Street.

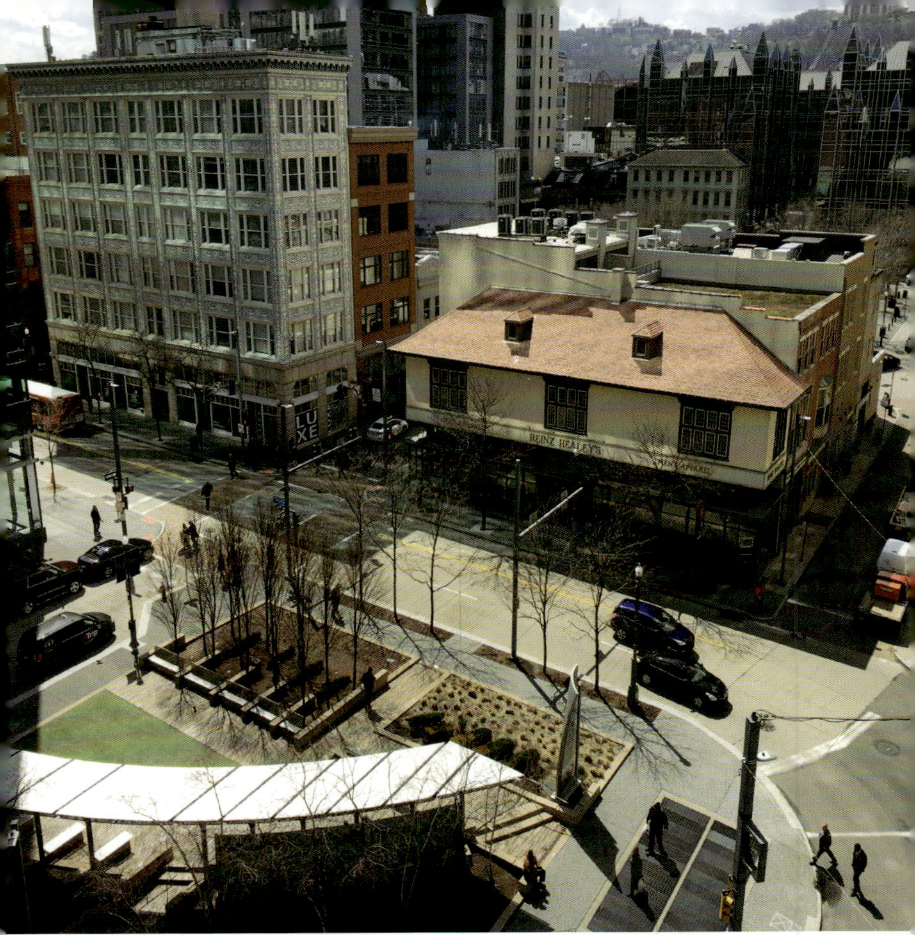
LUXE
HEINZ HEALEY'S

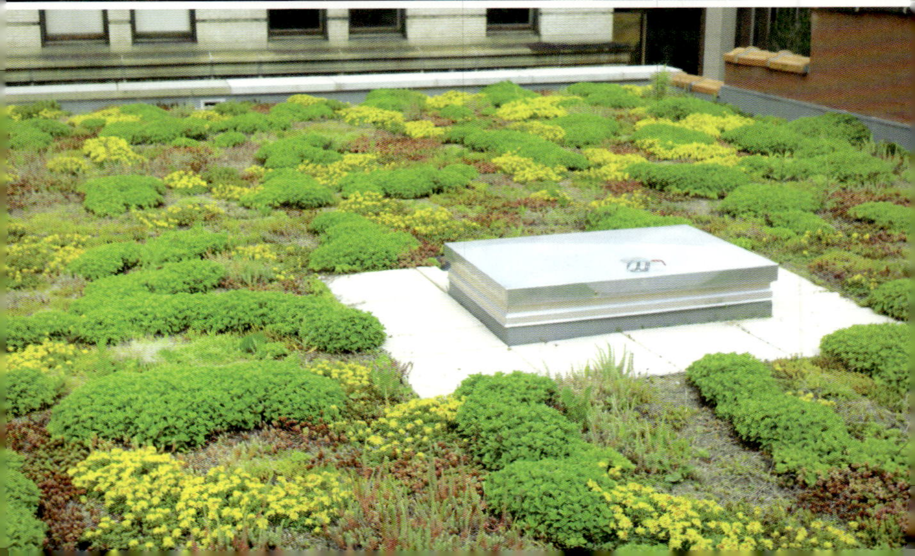

What's "Green" Downtown?

"Green building" addresses a building's design, construction, and operations through a variety of considerations, including location, linkages, site, reuse of structures, design, water efficiency, energy use, materials, indoor environmental quality, and innovation.

There are a number of green-building rating and certifications around the world, but the U.S. Green Building Council (USGBC)'s Leadership in Energy and Environmental Design (LEED) green-building rating system is the most prolific, certifying buildings at four levels: certified, silver, gold, or platinum. Pittsburgh boasts many ENERGY STAR and certified green buildings, with increasing numbers pursuing zero net energy, in line with the City's Climate Action Plan.

Notable Downtown Green Buildings
(in chronological order)

- **PNC Firstside Center** *(see page 15)*: the nation's first green financial institution (LEED for New Construction [NC] Silver, 2000)
- **David L. Lawrence Convention Center** *(see page 46)*: the world's first green convention center (LEED-NC Gold, 2003; LEED for Operations & Maintenance [O+M] Platinum, 2012 & 2017)
- **Senator John Heinz History Center, Smithsonian Wing** *(see page 83)*: the nation's first green Smithsonian property (LEED-NC Silver, 2005)
- **Point Park University Dance Complex**, 321 Boulevard of the Allies: the nation's first green university dance complex (LEED-NC Gold, 2008)

Opposite: Market at Fifth, Downtown Pittsburgh's first LEED Gold certified historic rehabilitation (2010), includes a green roof; two apartments have terraces looking out onto the roof *(see page 63)*.

- **PPG Paints Arena (originally Consol Energy Center)**, 1001 Fifth Avenue: the nation's first newly constructed National Hockey League facility (LEED-NC Gold, 2010)
- **William S. Moorhead Federal Building**, 1000 Liberty Avenue: a major renovation of a federal government building (LEED O+M Silver, 2013)
- **The Tower at PNC Plaza** *(see page 51)*: features a double-skin glass façade for natural ventilation and a solar chimney (LEED-NC Platinum, 2015)
- **Energy Innovation Center**, 1435 Bedford Avenue: a historic renovation living laboratory to support sustainable energy solutions and workforce development (LEED Core & Shell Platinum, 2017)
- **U.S. Steel Tower**: the seventh largest high-rise office building in the nation (ENERGY STAR, 2017; LEED-Commercial Interior [CI], 1 million+ square feet, since 2009)

Pittsburgh 2030 District

The Pittsburgh 2030 District is an internationally recognized, locally driven initiative that empowers, supports, and inspires business and building owners striving for 50 percent reductions in energy use, water consumption, and transportation emissions by 2030, while improving indoor air quality.

Established in 2012, the District connects more than 100 Property Partners with more than 40 Community and Resource Partners, driving industry-leading building performance through peer-to-peer learning, technical trainings, and data benchmarking. From its beginnings in Downtown, the 2030 District now stretches across Pittsburgh's urban core and includes more than 200 buildings in greater Downtown. The Pittsburgh 2030 District is a private-public-nonprofit partnership facilitated by Green Building Alliance (GBA). The Pittsburgh 2030 District annually reports its progress online at **2030district.org/pittsburgh**.

Appendix

Green Roofs in Downtown Pittsburgh
(in chronological order according to certification)

Green roofs absorb rainwater, reduce stormwater runoff, reduce heating and cooling costs, lengthen a roof's lifespan, and create vistas where there were previously none.

- **Heinz 57 Center** *(see page 38)*: a 15,000-square-foot green roof with 18,000 plants is on the penthouse level (2001)
- **Fifth Avenue Place** (Highmark; *see page 62)*: a 22,000-square-foot green roof with 25,000 plants is three stories above street level on the terrace at the corner of Liberty and Fifth avenues (2008)
- **Market at Fifth** *(see page 63)*: a 1,400-square-foot green roof is above the apartments facing Graeme Street (2010)
- **Allegheny County Office Building**, 542 Forbes Avenue: an 8,400-square-foot green roof faces Ross Street and serves as an educational model to demonstrate the benefits of green roofs (2010)

The green roof of the Allegheny County Office Building, just after planting in 2010

The south terrace of the David L. Lawrence Convention Center incorporates a green roof that also serves as an event space.

- **YWCA Greater Pittsburgh**, 305 Wood Street: a 4,900-square-foot green roof is four floors above Wood Street (2011)
- **David L. Lawrence Convention Center** *(see page 46)*: a 20,000-square-foot green roof features over 7,000 perennials, grasses, and sedum (2012)
- **Mellon Square** *(see page 37)*: a 1.37-acre Modernist park with a green roof, plantings, and water features is above street-level retail and an underground parking garage (1955, refreshed 2014)
- **The Tower at PNC Plaza** *(see page 51)*: there are green roofs on three levels (2015)

Information provided by Green Building Alliance: GBA advances innovation in the built environment by empowering people to create environmentally, economically, and socially vibrant places. Founded in 1993, GBA is an independent 501(c)(3) nonprofit organization—and one of the oldest regional green building organizations in the United States. GBA proudly serves Pittsburgh and the 26 counties of Western Pennsylvania, with stakeholders across the Mid-Atlantic, United States, and the world. **GBA.org**,

From the outdoor terrace on the third floor of The Tower at PNC Plaza, you can spy the heads of eagles and lions on two historic buildings at Wood Street and Forbes Avenue *(see pages 54–55)*. Market Square and Gateway Center are in the distance, to the west.

PITTSBURGH'S
LANDMARK
ARCHITECTURE
THE HISTORIC BUILDINGS OF PITTSBURGH AND ALLEGHENY COUNTY

Pittsburgh's Bridges
Architecture and Engineering

Henry Hornbostel
An Architect's Master Touch

Clyde Hare's Pittsburgh

BEYOND THE SURFACE

LIFE'S RICHES

August Wilson:
Pittsburgh Places in His Life and Plays

Pittsburgh Architecture
in the Twentieth Century
Notable Modern Buildings and Their Architects
Albert M. Tannler

H. H. Richardson's
Allegheny County
Courthouse & Jail
Guidebook
Albert M. Tannler

Charles J. Connick:
His Education and His Windows
in and near Pittsburgh
Albert M. Tannler

Pittsburgh History & Landmarks Foundation

Publications and Tours

Exploring Pittsburgh: A Downtown Walking Tour is one in a series of guidebooks published by the Pittsburgh History & Landmarks Foundation (PHLF). Other titles include:

- *H. H. Richardson's Allegheny County Courthouse & Jail Guidebook*, by Albert M. Tannler (2016)
- *August Wilson: Pittsburgh Places in His Life and Plays*, by Laurence A. Glasco and Christopher Rawson (2015)
- *Pittsburgh Architecture in the Twentieth Century: Notable Modern Buildings and Their Architects*, by Albert M. Tannler (2013)
- *Charles J. Connick: His Education and His Windows in and near Pittsburgh,* by Albert M. Tannler (2008)

To purchase these or other major books on Pittsburgh's history and architecture, please visit **www.phlf.org** and click on "Store." Or, e-mail **info@phlf.org** or phone 412-471-5808.

PHLF also offers a year-round, guided tour service for private groups or schools and a series of free guided walking tours that are open to the public. Visit **www.phlf.org** and click on "Tours & Events" for further information. Self-guided walking tour brochures are available at **www.phlf.org** (click on "Education" and then "Self-guided Walks") for the following areas in Downtown Pittsburgh:

- Gateway Center
- Grant Street
- Market Square Area
- Penn–Liberty
- Fourth Avenue
- Bridges & River Shores

Appendix

Two 30-foot-high curved oak doors open in First Presbyterian Church to reveal the south chancel window by Clayton & Bell of London, England. The church also includes 13 windows by Frederick Wilson of Tiffany Studios, New York; one window by Charles R. Lamb of New York; and the north façade window by William Willet of Pittsburgh.

Illustration Sources

All images are from the Pittsburgh History & Landmarks Foundation unless otherwise noted. Other sources, with corresponding page numbers, are listed here.

- Carnegie Library of Pittsburgh: 60 (both)
- David L. Lawrence Convention Center: 88
- Colin Hines: 45 (bottom right), 71 (bottom), 94 (top)
- Jim Judkis: 13 (top right), 78 (both), 104 (top left)
- B. Glenn Lewis: 20 (top right)
- Pittsburgh City Photographer Collection, Archives Service Center, University of Pittsburgh: 12
- Greg Pytlik: 90, 104 (bottom)
- William Rydberg, PHOTON: 14 (top right), 19 (right), 35 (bottom)
- John Schalcosky, Founder, Odd Pittsburgh: inside front and back cover photo of Pittsburgh from January 5, 1931
- VisitPITTSBURGH and maps.com: 8–9

Grand Lobby, Heinz Hall for the Performing Arts

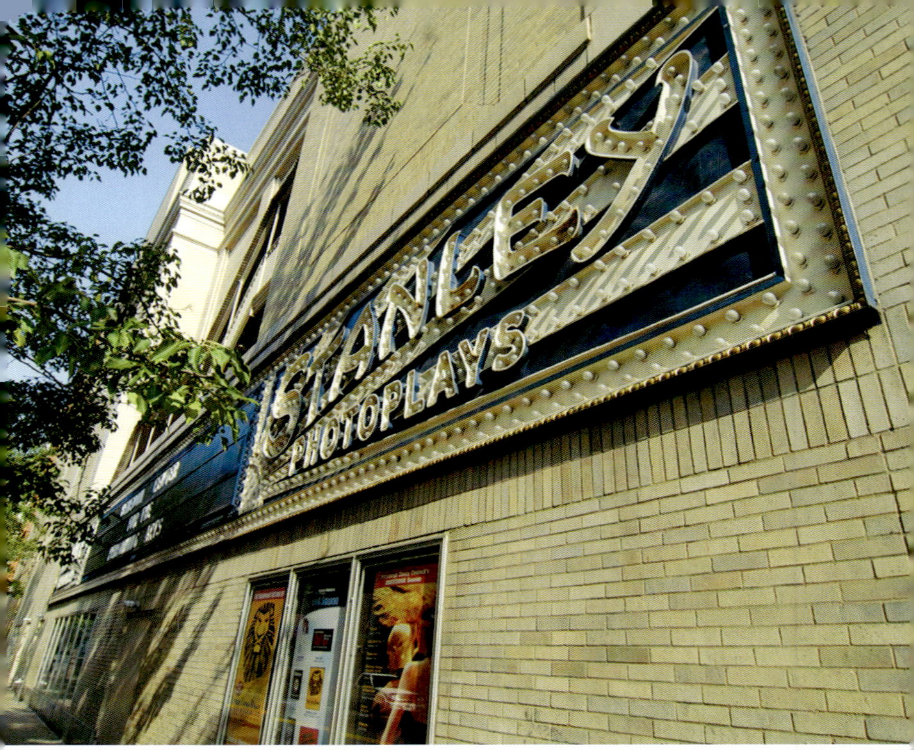
STANLEY
PHOTOPLAYS

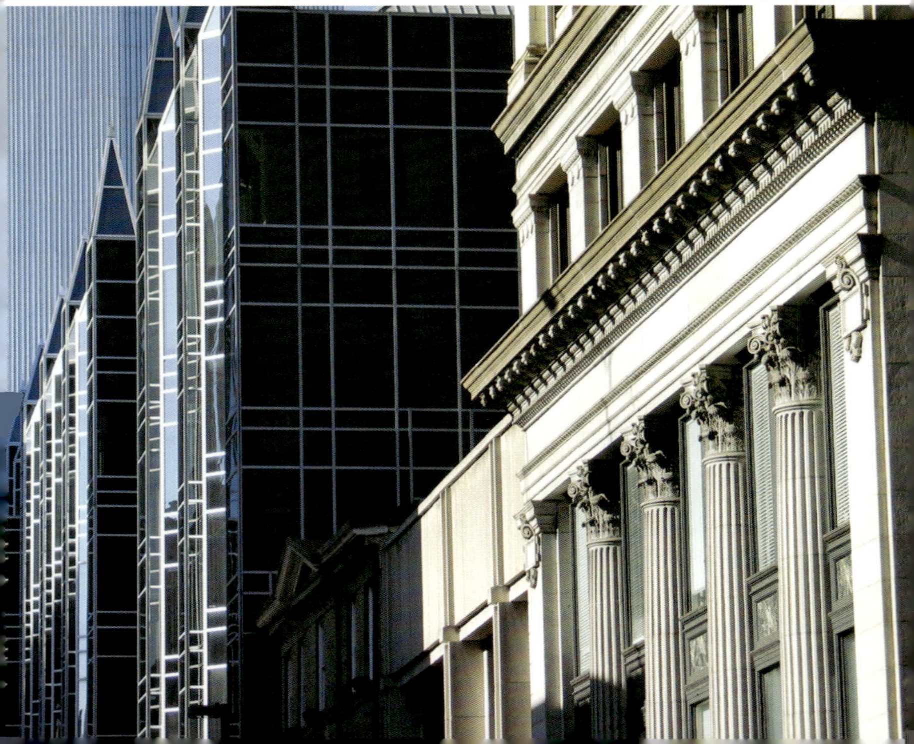

Bibliography

Aurand, Martin. *The Spectator and the Topographical City.* Pittsburgh: University of Pittsburgh Press, 2006.

Cleary, Richard L. *Merchant Prince and Master Builder: Edgar J. Kaufmann and Frank Lloyd Wright.* Seattle: Heinz Architectural Center, Carnegie Museum of Art in association with the University of Washington Press, 1999.

Donnelly, Lu et al. *Buildings of Pennsylvania: Pittsburgh and Western Pennsylvania.* Charlotte: University of Virginia Press (2010). A volume in the Buildings of the United States series of the Society of Architectural Historians.

Kidney, Walter C. *Henry Hornbostel: An Architect's Master Touch.* Pittsburgh: Pittsburgh History & Landmarks Foundation, 2002.

Kidney, Walter C. *Pittsburgh's Bridges: Architecture and Engineering.* Pittsburgh: Pittsburgh History & Landmarks Foundation, 1999.

Kidney, Walter C. *Pittsburgh's Landmark Architecture: The Historic Buildings of Pittsburgh and Allegheny County.* Pittsburgh: Pittsburgh History & Landmarks Foundation, 1997.

Lowry, Patricia. "What Were They Thinking? Pittsburgh Then & Now." Pittsburgh: *Pittsburgh Post-Gazette*, December 18, 2005.

PNC Realty Services. "The Tower at PNC Plaza: Self-Guided Tour." Pittsburgh: PNC Realty Services, no date.

Tannler, Albert M. *H. H. Richardson's Allegheny County Courthouse & Jail Guidebook.* Pittsburgh: Pittsburgh History & Landmarks Foundation, 2016.

Tannler, Albert M. *Pittsburgh Architecture in the Twentieth Century: Notable Modern Buildings and Their Architects.* Pittsburgh: Pittsburgh History & Landmarks Foundation, 2013.

Van Trump, James D. *Majesty of the Law: The Court Houses of Allegheny County.* Pittsburgh: Pittsburgh History & Landmarks Foundation, 1988.

Opposite: the Benedum Center for the Performing Arts (top), and PPG Place and the Benedum-Trees Building

ICE CREAM · WIENER WORLD · ICE CREAM
HOTDOGS · FRIES · KIELBASA · FISH · ICE CREAM · PIZZA · HOAGIES

The King's Garden:
Founding Pittsburgh in the 18th Century

FORT PITT

CALL AT THE POINT

Index

7-Eleven, 54
300 Sixth Avenue Building, 8, 48–49
400 Block, Wood Street, 8, 53–56
500 Smithfield, 38
525 William Penn Place, 38

Abbe, Charles H., 25
Abramovitz, Max, 25, 36, 38, 71
Alcoa, 36. *Also see* The Residences at the Historic Alcoa Building
Alden & Harlow, 34, 41, 63, 64, 67, 69
Allegheny County Court of Common Pleas (Family Division), 13, 83
Allegheny County Courthouse and Jail, i, iii, 8, 10–13, 14, 19, 20, 21, 25, 26, 70, 73
Allegheny County Jail Museum, 13, 83
Allegheny County Office Building, 87
Allegheny HYP Club, 8, 36
Arrott Building, 67
Astorino, 15, 65
Atterbury, Grosvenor, 46
August Wilson Center—African American Cultural Center (August Wilson Center for African American Culture), 48, 83
Aurand, Martin, 4

Bank Tower, 67
Bartberger, Charles M., 68
Bash Building, 64
Bearden, Romare, 43, 102
Bell Telephone Building, 34
Benedum Center for the Performing Arts, 45–46, 95
Benedum-Trees Building, 66–67, 95
Berke, Arnold, i
Berry, Stephen, 73
Bickel, Charles, 42, 47, 48
Bickel & Brennan, 42
BNY Mellon Center, 8, 22, 24–25
BNY Mellon Green, 4, 24–25
Bossom, Alfred C., 46
Bouquet, Colonel Henry, 75
Bourgeois, Louise, 46
Bower Lewis Thrower, 29
Brangwyn, Cuthbert P., 49
Brangwyn, Frank, 49
Brennan, John P., 42
Brubach, Holly, 42
Buhl Building, 8, 58, 64
Bunshaft, Gordon, 49, 77
Burke's Building, 3, 8, 66
Burnham, D. H. & Company, 10, 17, 20, 29, 32, 38, 48, 68
Burt Hill Kosar Rittelmann, 25
Burton, Scott, 25
Byham Theater, 46, 47

Opposite (top to bottom): The ornate terra-cotta roofs of the Union Trust Building (Grant Street); a whimsical mural of Andy Warhol and Andrew Carnegie by Tom Mosser and Sarah Zeffiro (Smithfield Street and Strawberry Way); and a map of Fort Pitt on the Café at the Point, designed in 2011 by Pfaffmann + Associates (Point State Park)

Index

Campbell, Jim, 43
Carnegie, Andrew, 18, 97
Carpenter & Crocker, 39
Celli-Flynn Associates, 22
Chandler, Theophilus Parsons, 40
Chislett, John, 66
City-County Building, vii, ix, 8, 11, 13–14
Clarke + Rapuano, 72
Clavan, Irwin, 72
Clayton & Bell, 40, 92
CNG Tower, 62
Colonial Trust Company, 57
Commonwealth Trust Company, 68
Cook, Howard, 27
Courtyard Pittsburgh Downtown, 46, 47
Crosby, H. E., 58
Cultural District, 8, 45–48
CVS/pharmacy, 8, 57

Damianos, Sylvester, 56
David L. Lawrence Convention Center, 46, 47, 85, 88
de Blois, Natalie, 49–50
Dick, Sir William Reid, 14
Distrikt Hotel Pittsburgh, 16
Dollar Bank, 69
Dominion Tower, 62
Donahoe's Market and Cafeteria, 57
Donn, John M., 67
Drury Plaza Hotel Pittsburgh Downtown, 8, 30-31
Duquesne Club, 8, 41
Duquesne Incline, i, 83

Eggers & Higgins, 72
Embassy Suites by Hilton Pittsburgh Downtown, 38
EQT Plaza, 62
Equibank, 49
Exchange National Bank Building, 59

Fairmont Pittsburgh, 65
Federal Courthouse and Post Office, 27
Federal Reserve Bank of Cleveland, Pittsburgh Branch, 30
Fifth Avenue Place, 62, 87
Fifth Wood Building, 53
First Lutheran Church, 8, 26–27
First Presbyterian Church, 8, 40, 92
Forbes, British General John, 23, 73
Fort Duquesne, 73, 75
Fort Pitt, 61, 74
Fort Pitt Block House, 3, 75, 83
Fort Pitt Museum, 75, 83
Four Gateway Center, 8, 71
Fourth Avenue Historic District, 8, 66–69
Fownes, H. C., 42
Freyssinet, Eugène, 77
Frick, Henry Clay, 17–20, 21
Frick Building, 8, 10, 17–20
Fulton Building, 46

Gateway Center One, Two, and Three, 4, 8, 72
G. C. Murphy Company Building, 58
Gensler, 51, 65
German National Bank, 42

Goldsmith, Myron, 49
Goodhue, Bertram, 4, 39
Graham, Anderson, Probst & White, 32
Granite Building, 8, 42
Grant Building, 8, 14–15
Grant's Hill, 12, 20
Gratz, Roberta Brandes, 72
Graves, Michael, 5, 46
Great Fire (1845), 2, 3, 62, 66
Green Building Alliance, 86, 88
Griswold, Ralph E., 73, 75
Guastavino, Rafael, 12
Guibara, Albert, 16
Gulf Tower (Building), 8, 27, 32

Hannah, Thomas, 44
Harris, Charles "Teenie," 48
Harris Theater, 46, 47
Harrison & Abramovitz, 25, 36, 38, 71
Harriton Carved Glass Company, 49
Heinz 57 Center, 38, 87
Heinz Hall for the Performing Arts, 45, 93
Heinz History Center (Senator John), 83, 85
Hellmuth, Obata, Kassabaum, 17
Henry E. Sharp Studio, 39
Henry W. Oliver Building, 19, 38
Hering, Henry, 30
Highmark, 62, 87
Hilton hotels, 73
Hobbs, Isaac, 69
Hoffman, Malvina, 20
Hornbostel, Henry, 5, 13–14, 30, 35

Hugh Stubbins Associates, 62
Hunt Stained Glass Studios, 39
Hunting, Davis & Dunnells, 54
Hutchins, William P., 71

IKM Incorporated, 13, 43
Industrial Bank, 68
Investment Building, 67
Italian Sons and Daughters of America, 54–55

Janssen, Benno, 5
Janssen & Abbott, 22, 63, 64
Janssen & Cocken, 22, 41
J. G. Johnson Architects, 46
John M. Roberts & Son Company, 54
Johnson, Philip, 5, 70
Johnson/Burgee Architects, 70
Joseph F. Weis Jr. United States Courthouse, 8, 27

Karoly, Andrew, 23
Kashi Jewelers, 53
Katz (Agnes R.) Plaza, 4, 46
Kaufmann's Department Store, 42, 64
Kaufmann's Grand on Fifth Avenue, 42
KDKA Weather Beacon, 32
Keck, Charles, ix
Keenan Building, 44
Kidney, Walter C., iii, 62, 64, 79
Kiley, Daniel Urban, 46
Kimpton Hotel Monaco Pittsburgh, 38–39
Klavon Design Associates, 61
Kobet, Robert J., 66
Kohn Pedersen Fox, 62

Index

Koppers Building, 8, 32–34
Kuntz, Joseph F., 38–39

La Farge, John, 20
Lamb, Charles R., 40, 92
Landmarks Design Associates (LDA Architects), 63, 66
Landmarks Development Corporation (LDC), 55, 63, 81, 104
LaQuatra Bonci Associates, 65
Lee, Edward B., 13, 36
LEED (Leadership in Energy and Environmental Design), 15, 48, 51, 58, 63, 85–89
Lewis, David, x, 1, 5
LeWitt, Sol, 43
Lloyd, Gordon W., 39
Longfellow, Alden & Harlow, 5, 41
Lowry, Patricia, 72

MacClure & Spahr, 38, 67
MacLachlan, Cornelius & Filoni, 43, 48
Market at Fifth, 8, 58, 63–64, 81, 85, 87
Market Square, 4, 8, 52, 58, 59, 60–62
Market Square Place, 8, 58–59
McCreery & Company Department Store, 48–49
Meadmore, Clement, 16
Mellon, Andrew W., 27, 37
Mellon, E. P., 32, 38
Mellon, Richard Beatty, 37
Mellon Bank, 27, 38
Mellon Square, 4, 8, 22, 27, 37–38, 88

Midtown Towers, 8, 44
Millcraft Industries, Inc., 58
Mitchell, James A., 37
Mitchell & Ritchey, 37
Monongahela Bank, 43
Mosley, Thaddeus, 48
Mosser, Tom, 97
MTR Landscape Architects, 25

N & P Properties, 64
Nesbert, Vincent, 13
Nicola, Franklin, 64

Oakmont Country Club, 42, 43
O'Gorman, James F., 12
Oliver, Henry W., 18–19, 38, 48
Omni William Penn Hotel, 8, 17, 22–23
One Oxford Centre, 8, 17
One PNC Plaza, 8, 16, 50
O'Reilly Theater, 46, 47
Original Oyster House, 62
Osterling, Frederick J., 21, 34, 43, 56, 57, 67, 68

Paley, Albert, 43
Palmer, Hornbostel & Jones, 13
Park Building, 38
Parrendo, Nicholas, 39
Parsons Brinckerhoff, 43
Peebles, Andrew W., 26, 43
Penn family (heirs of William Penn), 3, 35, 40, 45, 61
Peoples Savings Bank Building, 67
Perfido Weiskopf Architects, 46
Perkins + Will (San Francisco, CA), 48
Pfaffmann + Associates, 97
Phipps, Henry, 18–19

Index

Phipps Pennsylvania Land Trust, 18–19, 46
Pitt (the Elder), Sir William, ix, 14, 73
Pittsburgh 2030 District, 86
Pittsburgh Bank for Savings, 69
Pittsburgh CAPA, 46, 47, 48
Pittsburgh Cultural Trust, 45
Pittsburgh Engineers' Building, 68
Pittsburgh History & Landmarks Foundation (PHLF), 13, 42, 53–56, 63, 64, 65, 66, 67, 81, 91, 104
Pittsburgh National Bank Building, 50
Pittsburgh Parks Conservancy, 37
Pittsburgh Playhouse (Point Park University), 5, 57, 68
PNC Firstside Center, 8, 15–16, 43, 85
PNC Firstside Park, 4, 8, 15–16
PNC Triangle Park, 4, 8, 65
Point Park University Center, 8, 56–57
Point State Park, 3, 8, 73–77, 97
Portal Bridge, 77
Post, George B., 27, 38
PPG Place (and Plaza), 4, 8, 61, 62, 66, 70, 71, 81, 95
Pressley Associates, Inc., 73
Primanti Brothers, 62
Pringle, Thomas, 16
Proctor, Alexander Phimister, 20

Rafael Viñoly Associates PC, 46
Rapp & Rapp, 45
Regal Shoe Company, 64
Regional Enterprise Tower, 37
Renaissance Pittsburgh Hotel, 19, 46, 47
Richardson, George S., 77
Richardson, Henry Hobson, i, iii, 4, 10, 11–13, 19, 21, 25, 26, 41, 70, 73
Riverlife, 75
Roush, Stanley L., 12
Rowland, George M., 54
Rutan & Russell, 41, 60

St. Mary of Mercy Church, 8, 71
Schell & Deeter, 71
Schenley, Mary Croghan, 44, 75
Schwan, George H., 53
Scott, Thomas H., 66
Simonds & Simonds, 37, 71
Skidmore, Owings & Merrill [SOM], 49–50, 77
"Skinny" Building, 53, 54
Smithfield United Church, 8, 35, 36, 37
Snaman, William E., 57
S. S. Marshall & Company, 26
Standard Life Building, 69
Starrett & Van Vleck, 38
Steen, James T., 69
Stickley, Gustav, 49
Stotz, Charles Morse, 73, 77
Stotz, Edward, 43, 77
Stotz, Hess, MacLachlan & Fosner, 45
Strada, 30, 36, 39, 58
Szanto, Louis, 23

"T" (transit station), 15, 25, 43, 102
Tabler, William B., Jr., 73

101

"Pittsburgh Recollections," by African-American artist Romare Bearden (1911–1988), is in the Gateway "T" Station in Downtown Pittsburgh. Created in 1984, the ceramic-tile mural shows Pittsburgh as a military outpost, frontier town, and industrial city. Bearden, pictured at the far right holding a paint brush, graduated from Pittsburgh's Peabody High School in 1929.

The Carlyle, 67
The Davis Companies, 21
The Pennsylvanian, 8, 28–29
The Residences at the Historic Alcoa Building, 8, 36–37
The Tower at PNC Plaza, 8, 51–52, 86, 88, 89
Theater Square, 46, 47
Thompsons Building (John R.), 63, 81
Thorvaldsen, Bertel, 27
Three PNC Plaza, 8, 58, 65
Tiffany Glass & Decorating Company, 27
Tiffany Studios, 40, 92

Times Building, 68
Trinity Cathedral, 8, 39, 40
Trowbridge & Livingston, 27, 32, 38
Two PNC Plaza, 8, 49–50
Tyler, Cindy, 25

Union National Bank, 67
Union Station, 29
Union Trust Building (Union Arcade), 8, 17, 21, 25, 97
Union Trust Company, 68
United States Steel Innovations Committee, 25
UPMC, 25

Urban, Joseph, 22
U.S. Green Building Council, 85
U.S. Steel Tower, 8, 25–26, 86

Van Rensselaer, Mariana G. S., 11
Van Trump, James D., 17, 18–19, 29
Van Veen, Stuveysant, 27
Verizon Building, 8, 34–35
Vickroy, Thomas, 3, 45
Von Gerichten, Ludwig, 35

Walker & Weeks, 30
Warhol, Andy, 83, 97
Washington, George, 23, 44, 74
Weary & Alford, 59
Weis, Joseph F., Jr., 27
Welton Becket & Associates, 22, 50
Wetmore, James A., 27

Willet, William and Anne Lee, 40
William Penn Hotel, 17, 22. *Also see* Omni William Penn Hotel
Williams, Allison, 48
Williams Trebilcock Whitehead, 62
Wilson, August, 48. *Also see* August Wilson Center—African American Cultural Center
Wilson, Frederick, 26–27, 40, 92
Windrim, James T., 34
Wood, Eric Fisher, 14, 30
Wood Street Building, 48
Wood Street Galleries, 8, 43
Wood Street Station, 8, 43
Woods, George, 3, 45
Wyndham Grand Pittsburgh Downtown, 8, 73

Zeffiro, Sarah, 97

Pittsburgh History & Landmarks Foundation
Renewing Communities; Building Pride

- Founded in 1964
- Headquartered in The Landmarks Building at Station Square
- At work throughout the Pittsburgh region
- Includes Landmarks Community Capital Corporation and Landmarks Development Corporation, both wholly-owned subsidiaries

Our trustees, staff, members, and volunteers work with others to:
- **identify and save** historically significant places;
- **revitalize** historic neighborhoods, towns, and urban areas;
- **preserve** historic farms and historic designed landscapes; and
- **educate** people about the region's rich architectural heritage.

To contribute or to become involved, visit **www.phlf.org**, call 412-471-5808, or e-mail **info@phlf.org**. We welcome your support.